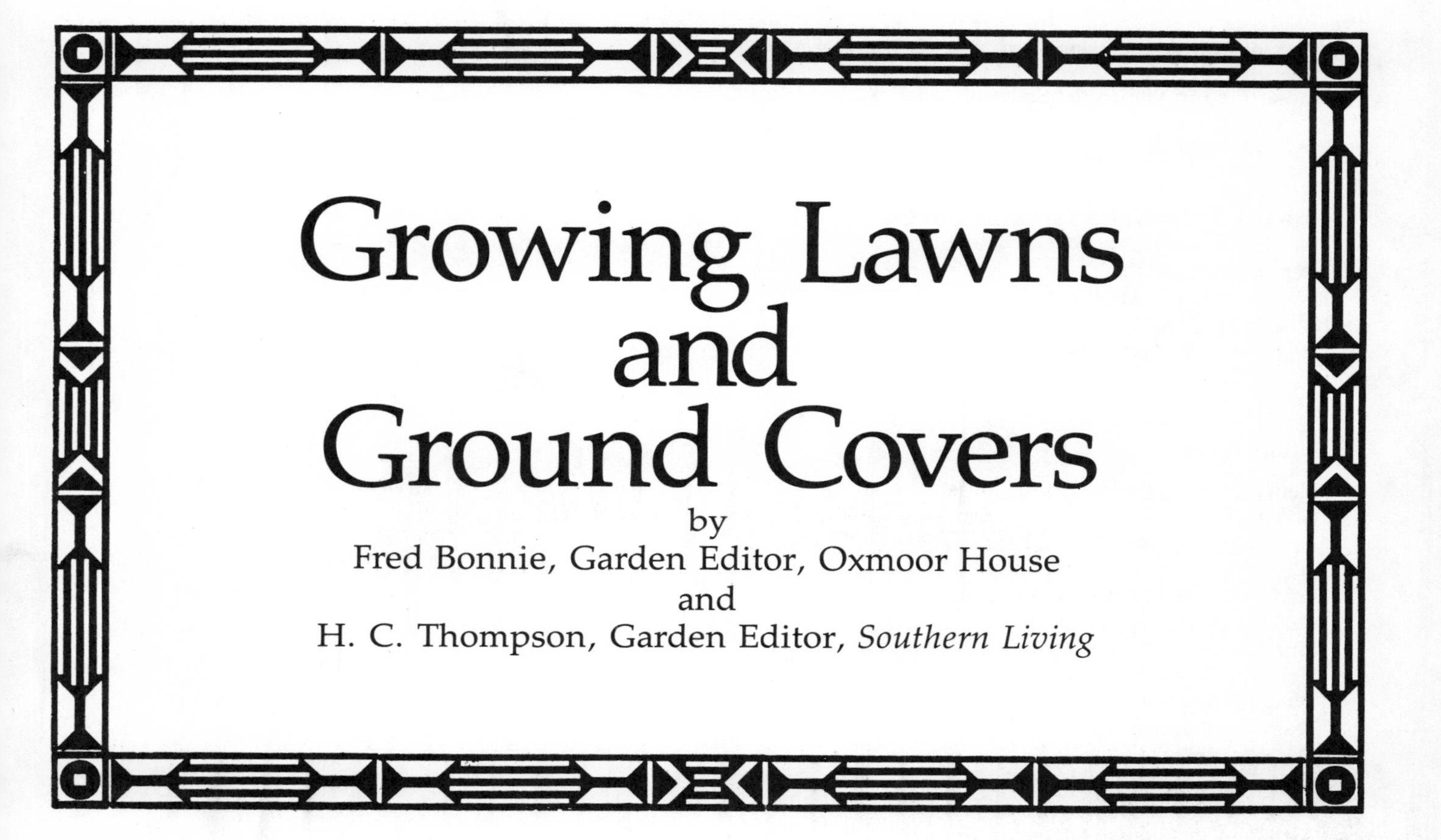

Growing Lawns and Ground Covers

by
Fred Bonnie, Garden Editor, Oxmoor House
and
H. C. Thompson, Garden Editor, *Southern Living*

Book Division of The Progressive Farmer Company
P.O. Box 2463, Birmingham, Alabama 35202

Library of Congress Catalog Card Number: 75–12125

Manufactured in the United States of America

First Printing 1975

Growing Lawns and Ground Covers

Cover: Taylor Lewis
Illustrations: Ralph Mark
Photography: Jack Goodson, Bob Lancaster,
Joe Benton, Bert O'Neal

Introduction

The availability of powered groundskeeping equipment for the homeowner has made possible the planting and maintenance of sizable lawns. An acre of lawn can now be mowed in an hour or two, and you can sit down while you're doing it. Forty years ago a lawn one-fourth that size would have been unthinkable, except to an exceptionally enthusiastic few.

But not everyone wants such a large lawn. Some people may not want to spend even one hour a week mowing a lawn. Many homeowners, though they would like to spend more time working in the yard, simply do not have the time. For the low-maintenance gardener, ground cover may be the answer. Most ground covers are easy to establish (which is why they have been selected as desirable plants for this purpose) and easy to maintain, usually requiring no more than one or two applications of fertilizer during the growing season and an annual clipping to keep them in bounds. Every 3 to 5 years, it may be necessary to thin the bed so that plants don't become crowded and stunted.

For most properties, a combination of lawn and ground cover will effectively provide contrast and interest in plant texture, color, and design. *Growing Lawns and Ground Covers* will help the homeowner or the professional landscaper in selecting, planting, and maintaining lawn grasses and ground cover plants for the home. A plant hardiness map and several charts of cultural requirements of plants provide information at a glance. Step-by-step instructions are provided throughout the book, and the glossary of garden terms will clarify any technical terminology you may not understand.

PLANT HARDINESS ZONE MAP

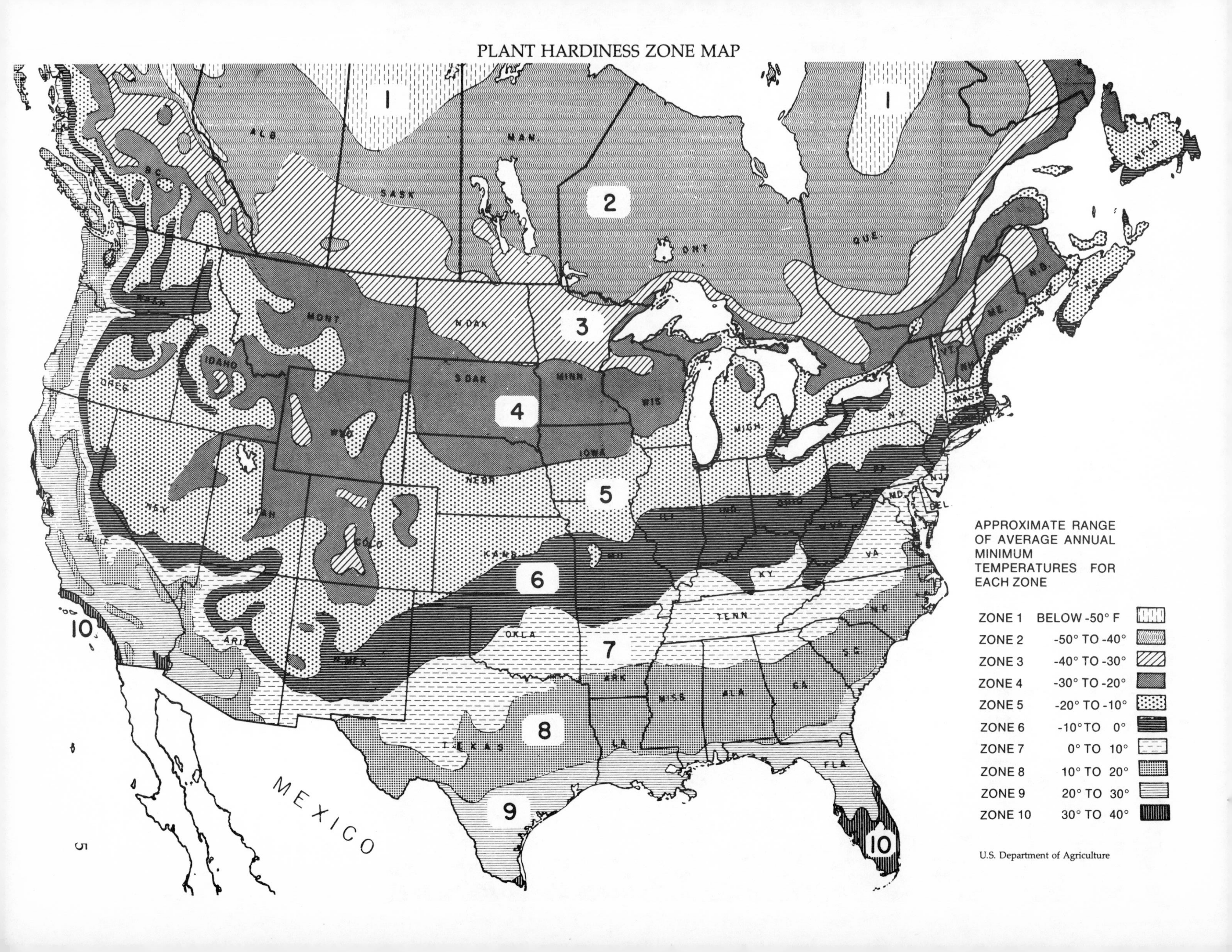

U.S. Department of Agriculture

Selecting the Right Grass

Lawns are so common today that one would think they appeared by spontaneous generation, growing automatically out of the soil around our homes. Anyone who has ever built a lawn can assure you that this is not the case. A beautiful lawn requires careful soil preparation and grass selection and regular, conscientious care.

A well-built lawn is truly beautiful. Nothing gives the home grounds as neat and manicured an appearance as a thick, lush carpet of green lawn. No plants tolerate being walked on, run on, played on, and generally lived on like lawn grasses. It is livability as well as beauty that makes the appeal of a fine lawn.

As with other types of plants, lawn grasses must be selected on the basis of their cultural requirements. Some lawn grasses tolerate shade, others thrive in it, and still others deteriorate and die in it. Sun exposure, then, is the first consideration. Other important factors include climate, moisture, soil type, and the amount of care required to keep the lawn looking its best. Finally, some grasses, such as common Bermuda, are more wear-resistant than others. If you expect a lot of foot traffic on the lawn, select a rugged grass.

To establish an attractive lawn, you must either select the grass best suited to your particular growing conditions or else modify existing conditions to meet the requirements of the grass you wish to grow. You may need to cut down a tree or at least thin out some branches to allow more light on your lawn area. If water tends to collect where you want to grow a lawn, you will need to improve drainage. These are just two general examples of the modifications you can make. More on these and other modifications later.

Types of Grasses

Lawn grasses are divided into 2 groups: warm-season and cool-season. Examples of warm-season grasses are bahia, the Bermudas, carpet, centipede, St. Augustine, and zoysias. Included in the cool-season grasses are bluegrass and the fescues.

Warm-season grasses begin their growth in early spring, grow vigorously throughout summer and early fall, and enter a period of nongrowth (called dormancy) with the first killing frost. These grasses thrive on hot weather.

Cool-season grasses, as the name implies, grow best in areas where snow frequently covers the ground all winter. In the Northeast, the Midwest, and southern Canada, lawns are grown with cool-season grasses. This is also true of the mountainous regions of the West and Upper South.

Along the Pacific Coast and in the Lower and Middle South, permanent lawns should be planted with warm-season grasses. The use of cool-season grasses in these areas is limited to temporary winter lawns, deep shade areas, or higher elevations. In the Upper South, a transitional zone, both cool-season and warm-season grasses are grown. Cool-season grasses, however, have the longer growing season in such marginal areas where they remain green most of the year.

Warm-season lawn grasses

Bahia

Bahia, though not the best turfgrass, is inexpensive and easy to establish and maintain. It has few insect and disease problems and is moderately wear-resistant. Frequent mowing is necessary to remove the tall seed heads. It spreads by short, thick underground stems, forming a dense turf with an extensive, deep root system, even in sandy soils. For this reason, bahia performs well in Florida and in the lower coastal areas. Its winter hardiness is comparable to that of carpet, centipede, and St. Augustine.

Bermuda

Bermudagrass is the most widely adapted of the southern lawn grasses. Although there is considerable difference in the appearance and growth characteristics of the various species and varieties of Bermudagrasses, as a group they are relatively vigorous, fine-textured, and dense growing.

Frequent feeding, watering, and careful mowing are essential to bring out the best in the Bermudas. They require more fertilization, especially with nitrogen, than other warm-season

Nothing gives the home a neat and yet casual atmosphere like a well-kept lawn.

Select lawn grasses according to climate tolerance, light needs, and maintenance requirements.

turfgrasses. The closer and more frequently Bermuda is mowed, the denser and more attractive the lawn. Because this grass spreads by both underground stems (rhizomes) and above ground runners (stolons), it is difficult to contain. Bermuda, however, is a rugged grass that stands up well in children's play areas.

Carpet

Carpetgrass is especially well adapted to sandy soils, particularly where moisture is near the surface.

It is identified by flat, two-edged runners or stolons and by large, coarse leaves with blunt tips. Relatively low-growing, carpetgrass forms a dense turf. It is recommended for lawns where ease of maintenance is more important than quality. Numerous tall seed heads that are produced all summer are the most objectionable characteristic of carpetgrass. Unless the grass is mowed frequently, these seed heads give the lawn an untidy appearance.

Centipede

Centipedegrass requires almost no feeding and less mowing than most grasses. Because it is well adapted to low-fertility soils, centipede has become popular as a lawn grass in certain sections of the South, especially in northern Florida, southern Georgia, and along the lower Gulf Coast as far west as Texas. Centipede is tolerant of filtered shade, heat, and drought.

Centipede spreads by means of thick, short-jointed, above ground runners that form a dense turf. Because it is low-growing, centipede is easy to maintain. It is moderately free of serious insect and disease problems. It does, however, have a tendency to develop serious iron deficiency.

St. Augustine

Compared to the many fine-textured lawn grasses in the South, St. Augustine is very coarse. Nevertheless, it remains a favorite with many people.

Well-cared-for St. Augustine grass establishes readily from above ground runners and forms a fairly dense, deep turf. Although it is aggressive and crowds out most other grasses and weeds, it is easy to keep in bounds. St. Augustine's best characteristic is its exceptional shade tolerance; it is the most shade tolerant of any warm-season lawn grass.

St. Augustine is adapted to a wide variety of soils, ranging from sand to clay, from moderately acid to alkaline. With the exception of being susceptible to chinch bugs and brown patch, St. Augustine is relatively easy to maintain. In recent years a virus disease, St. Augustine decline, has taken its toll of this grass in some areas of Texas. The variety 'Floratam' is resistant to this virus but is less cold-hardy than common St. Augustine.

Zoysia

Anyone who sees a well-managed lawn of

For lushness and durability, the new hybrid Bermudagrasses are difficult to surpass.

zoysia will usually agree that this grass, like the improved Bermudas, is truly an aristocrat among fine grasses. It spreads by surface runners and forms a dense, low-growing, compact turf.

An important growth characteristic of zoysiagrass is its ability to grow in light to medium shade. As shade is increased, however, the rate of growth is slowed. Also, the farther north it is planted, the slower zoysia grows, even in full sun. Slow growth has its advantages; once the zoysia lawn is established it will require less maintenance than a faster growing grass.

Zoysiagrasses are used for lawns and other fine turf areas where speed of establishment is secondary to quality. All existing vegetation should be destroyed prior to planting. Planting plugs of zoysia in an existing turf is not recommended. Early, close mowing with a sharp, reel-type power mower can speed establishment of this grass.

Cool-season lawn grasses

Bentgrass

Considered the best of the cool-season grasses, bentgrasses are used for lawns and golf greens from Newfoundland and Quebec south to Tennessee and west to Michigan. Bentgrass is the finest textured and densest growing grass used for turf. Suited to either full sun or partial shade, bentgrasses need moist, fertile soil that is acid in reaction; a pH of 5.0 to 5.5 is ideal. Its care is more demanding than that required for most lawn grasses. Maintenance of the correct soil pH, faithful, close mowing, and careful thatch control are all necessary for growing healthy bentgrass lawns. Bentgrasses are also more prone to chemical injury than most lawn grasses. Caution should be exercised in applying fertilizers and pesticides.

Bluegrass

Kentucky bluegrass spreads by means of underground stems and is the basic lawn grass of the cool, humid regions of the United States. In sunny areas of the Lower and Middle South, bluegrass becomes a cool-season annual, dying in the heat of midsummer. This grass provides a year-round lawn as far south as zone 7 and as far north as zone 2.

Fescue

The two major types of fescue used for lawns are red fescue and tall fescue. From zone 2 to the upper fringes of zone 8 they may be used for permanent lawns or similar turf areas. They are particularly recommended for shady areas and for higher altitudes. In the lower areas of its range of adaptation red fescue remains green year-round. Under warm, humid, full sun conditions of the Lower South, the fescues act as winter annuals and can be used only for temporary lawns during cool weather.

Seed Mixtures

The most beautiful lawn results when only a single kind of grass is used. Because of different light exposures or variations in soil structure, however, it is often beneficial to use a mixture of 2 or more types of seed. A vigorous-growing variety may be mixed with a slow-growing variety to quickly establish a grass cover. The slow grower may then crowd out the fast grower to establish a more permanent cover. Or, in sections of the South and West where lawns can be grown year-round, a mixture of cool-season and warm-season grasses will assure a green lawn throughout the year.

Mixtures of grass seed are available commercially. Should you wish to mix seed yourself, it may be wise to consult your county agricultural extension agent to find out which mixtures are best adapted to your area.

How to Buy Lawn Seed

When you buy lawn seed, read the label carefully. You'll want to look for these facts on the label:

1) A statement identifying the mixture of lawn seed as either fine-textured or coarse
2) The name and percentage of each kind of seed
3) The percentage of germination
4) The name of the variety
5) The percentage of weed seed

A variety is a subdivision of a type. For instance, 'Merion' is a variety of Kentucky bluegrass. The Federal Seed Act requires that variety names appearing on the label must be correct. You should select only varieties recommended by local experts.

The Federal Seed Act prohibits false labeling or advertising. You are further protected by state laws which require that the label on a container of lawn seed bear truthful and adequate information about the quality of the seed.

REGIONS OF GRASS ADAPTATION

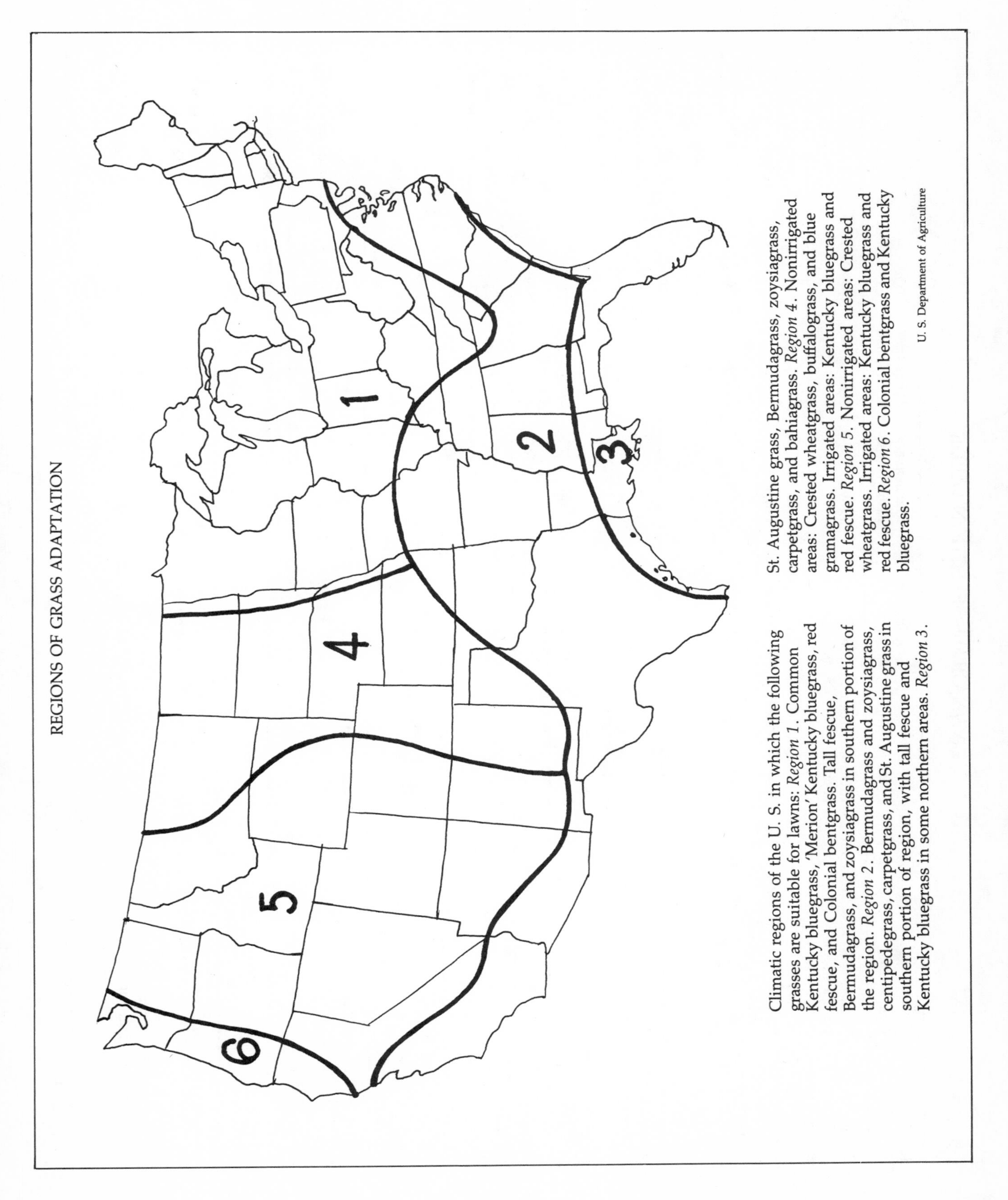

Climatic regions of the U. S. in which the following grasses are suitable for lawns: *Region 1*. Common Kentucky bluegrass, 'Merion' Kentucky bluegrass, red fescue, and Colonial bentgrass. Tall fescue, Bermudagrass, and zoysiagrass in southern portion of the region. *Region 2*. Bermudagrass and zoysiagrass, centipedegrass, carpetgrass, and St. Augustine grass in southern portion of region, with tall fescue and Kentucky bluegrass in some northern areas. *Region 3*. St. Augustine grass, Bermudagrass, zoysiagrass, carpetgrass, and bahiagrass. *Region 4*. Nonirrigated areas: Crested wheatgrass, buffalograss, and blue gramagrass. Irrigated areas: Kentucky bluegrass and red fescue. *Region 5*. Nonirrigated areas: Crested wheatgrass. Irrigated areas: Kentucky bluegrass and red fescue. *Region 6*. Colonial bentgrass and Kentucky bluegrass.

U. S. Department of Agriculture

LAWN GRASS SELECTION GUIDE

Type and Variety	*Light Needs*	*Rate of Spread*	*Color/Texture*	*Mowing Height/ Frequency*	*Maintenance Requirements*	*When Established*	*How Established*	*Rate per 1,000 sq. ft.*
Bahia	Sun or partial shade	Moderate	Medium green; coarse	2″ to 3″ weekly	Low	Spring	Seed	3 to 5 lbs.
Bent								
'Highland'	Sun or partial shade	Slow	Grayish green; fine	¾″ weekly	High	Spring	Seed	1 to 2 lbs.
'Pencross'	Sun or partial shade	Medium	Bluish green; fine	½″ weekly	High	Spring	Seed	1 to 2 lbs.
'Seaside'	Sun or partial shade	Fast	Bluish green; fine	½″ weekly	High	Spring	Seed	1 to 2 lbs.
Bermuda								
Common	Full sun	Very fast	Medium green; medium	1″ to 1½″ weekly	Low to medium	Spring or summer	Seed	2 to 3 lbs. (hulled) 5 lbs. (unhulled)
'No-Mow'	Sun or partial shade	Fast	Very dark green; fine	½″ to 1″ weekly	High	Spring	Sprigs Plugs Sod	4 to 6 sq. ft. on 12″ centers; 30 sq. ft. on 12″ centers
'Ormond'	Full sun	Fast	Dark blue green; medium	½″ to 1″ twice a week	High	Spring	Sprigs Plugs Sod	Same as above Same as above
'Sunturf'	Full sun	Very fast	Dark green; very fine	½″ to 1″ twice a week	High	Spring	Sprigs Plugs Sod	Same as above Same as above
'Texturf' 10	Full sun	Very fast	Dark green; medium	½″ to 1″ twice a week	High	Spring	Sprigs Plugs Sod	Same as above Same as above
'Tifgreen'	Full sun	Very fast	Dark green; very fine	½″ to 1″ twice a week	High	Spring	Sprigs Plugs Sod	Same as above Same as above
'Tiflawn'	Full sun	Very fast	Dark green; fine	½″ to 1″ twice a week	High	Spring	Sprigs Plugs Sod	Same as above Same as above
'Tifway'	Full sun	Very fast	Dark green; fine	½″ to 1″ twice a week	High	Spring	Sprigs Plugs Sod	Same as above Same as above

LAWN GRASS SELECTION GUIDE

Type and Variety	*Light Needs*	*Rate of Spread*	*Color/Texture*	*Mowing Height/ Frequency*	*Maintenance Requirements*	*When Established*	*How Established*	*Rate per 1,000 sq. ft.*
Kentucky Bluegrass Common	Sun or partial shade	Fast	Medium blue green; medium	2″ to 2½″ weekly	Medium	Fall	Seed	2 to 3 lbs.
'Merion'	Sun or partial shade	Fast	Dark blue green; medium	1½″ to 2½″ weekly	Medium	Fall	Seed	1 to 2 lbs.
Carpet	Sun or partial shade	Moderate to slow	Medium green; coarse	1½″ to 2″ weekly	Medium	Spring	Seed	3 to 5 lbs.
Centipede	Full sun or partial shade	Moderate	Medium to light green; coarse	1″ to 1½″ every 2 weeks	Low	Spring or summer	Seed Sprigs	¼ to ½ lb. 15 to 20 sq. ft. on 12″ centers
Fescue, Red	Sun or shade	Fast	Dark green; very fine	2″ to 2½″ weekly	Medium	Fall	Seed	2 to 4 lbs.
St. Augustine Common	Sun or shade	Moderate to fast	Medium green; coarse	1½″ to 2½″ weekly	Medium	Spring or summer	Sprigs	15 to 20 sq. ft. on 12″ centers; 30 sq. ft. on 12″ centers
'Floratam'	Sun or shade	Moderate	Blue green; medium	1½″ to 2″ weekly	Medium	Spring	Sprigs Plugs Sod	Same as above Same as above
Zoysia 'Emerald'	Sun or shade	Slow	Dark green; fine	½″ to 1½″ weekly	Medium	Spring	Sprigs Plugs Sod	15 to 20 sq. ft. on 6″ centers. 120 sq. ft. on 6″ centers
'Matrella'	Sun or shade	Very slow	Medium green; fine	½″ to 1½″ weekly	Medium	Spring	Sprigs Plugs Sod	Same as above Same as above
'Meyer'	Sun or shade	Slow	Dark green; medium	½″ to 1½″ weekly	Medium	Spring	Sprigs Plugs Sod	Same as above Same as above

Installing a New Lawn

Preparing the Soil

There is no easy way to build a new lawn. Shortcuts, if there are any, tend to result in a shoddy, uneven lawn that may never become well established and which may be easily eroded if your lawn area slopes. The basic steps in building a lawn are tilling, fertilizing, grading, planting (seeding, sodding, etc.), rolling, mulching, and watering. The lawn is a permanent landscape feature. Because of this, adequate preparation of the lawn area is crucial. Don't attempt to plant the lawn until you are satisfied that the soil is well drained and tilled to a depth of 6 to 10 inches with the correct amount of fertilizer and lime to assure healthy, rapid growth.

Collecting soil to be tested

Collect a pint of soil from the lawn area for analysis at the soil testing laboratory of your state department of agriculture or land grant college. Though this may seem an unnecessary step in the process of building a lawn, it can save you time, energy, and possibly money in purchasing fertilizer, lime, and other soil amendments. Call the office of your county agricultural extension agent for details on collecting and sending a soil sample. You can find the telephone number in the directory under your county government. Some garden supply centers test soil, too.

Tilling

Preparation of the lawn bed begins with a thorough turning of the soil. If you are building the lawn in the spring, wait until the soil is dry before attempting to turn it. To determine if the soil is dry enough to turn, dig some soil from the

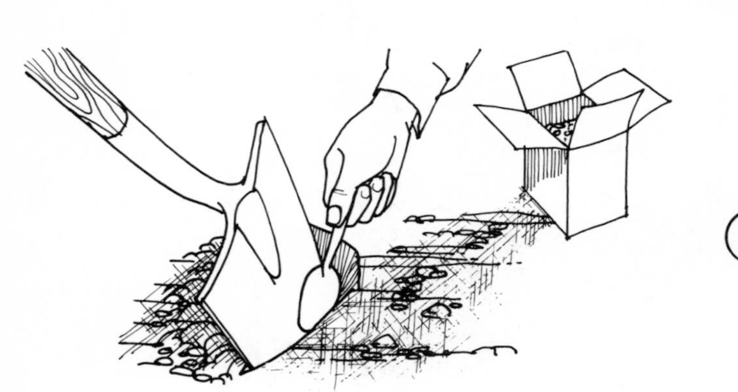

The county agricultural extension agent, listed in the telephone directory under county government, can send a container and instructions for collecting soil samples to be tested.

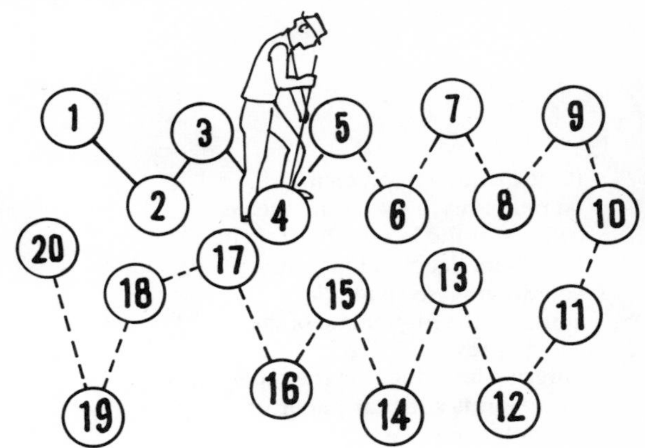

Collect 1 teaspoon of soil from 20 spots in the lawn area to fill the 1-pint soil sample container. Take samples in a zigzag and mix them thoroughly together.

REPORT ON SOIL TESTS
AUBURN UNIVERSITY
SOIL TESTING LABORATORY
AUBURN, ALABAMA 36830

PAGE

NAME FERN EBERHARD
ADDRESS 21 MOCKINGBIRD CT.
CITY McCALLA, ALABAMA

COUNTY JEFFERSON
DISTRICT 4
DATE 06/18/74

LAB NO.	SENDER'S SAMPLE DESIGNATION	SOIL* GROUP	SOIL TEST RESULTS					CROP TO BE GROWN	RECOMMENDATIONS				
			pH**	PHOSPHORUS P***	POTASSIUM K***	MAGNESIUM Mg***	CALCIUM Ca***		LIME-STONE TONS/ACRE	TO SUPPLY Mg	N (POUNDS PER ACRE)	P_2O_5 (POUNDS PER ACRE)	K_2O (POUNDS PER ACRE)
47368 1	1	2	5.8	EH3500	VH 290	H 830	****	ST AUGUSTINE	0.0		80	0	0

COMMENT 111.
PHOSPHOROUS IS EXCESSIVE AND FERTILIZERS CONTAINING THIS ELEMENT SHOULD NOT BE USED. EXCESSIVE PHOSPHOROUS MAY CAUSE AN IRON DEFICIENCY. THE SYMPTOMS OCCUR AS A GENERAL YELLOWING OF NEW GROWTH. TO CORRECT, SPRAY WITH A SOLUBLE SOURCE OF IRON WHICH CAN BE FOUND AT GARDEN SUPPLY STORES. USE AS DIRECTED

COMMENT 36.
PER 1,000 SQ. FT. APPLY 1 LB. N (3 LB. AMMONIUM NITRATE OR EQUIVALENT) WHEN SPRING GROWTH BEGINS AND REPEAT IN MID-SUMMER. IF MORE GROWTH OR BETTER COLOR IS DESIRED MAKE ADDITIONAL APPLICATIONS OF 1 LB. N AT 2-MONTH INTERVALS.

THE NUMBER OF SAMPLES PROCESSED IN THIS REPORT IS 1.

(SAMPLE OF A SOIL TEST REPORT)

* 1. Sandy soils
2. Loams & light clays
3. Heavy clays of the Blackbelt
4. Sandy loams of North Alabama
5. Heavy red clays of the limestone valleys

** 7.4 or higher Alkaline
6.6 -7.3 Neutral
6.5 or lower Acid
5.5 or lower Very acid

*** Rating & fertility index (percent sufficiency)

APPROVED

SOIL TESTING FORM B

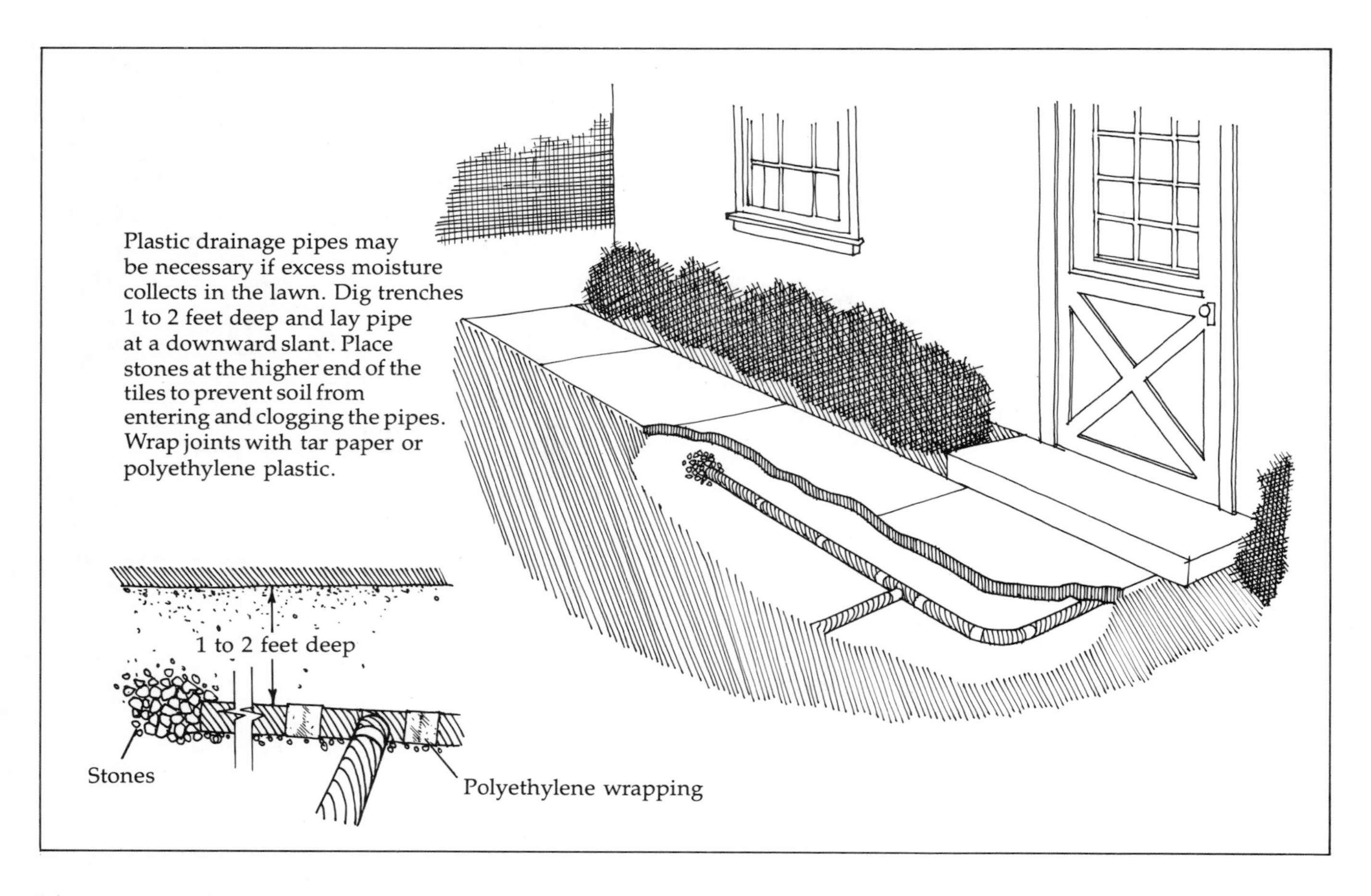

lawn area and squeeze a handful of it into a ball. If the soil sticks together in a ball, it is too wet. If it crumbles, it is dry enough to turn.

The best tool for turning the soil is a rotary tiller (also called a roto-tiller). In most communities, you can rent a tiller from a garden supply center or from a general rental agency. Till the soil thoroughly to a depth of 6 to 10 inches. This will require more than one pass with the tiller. Till until the soil is uniformly crumbly and all traces of old turf are thoroughly broken up. Some lawn experts recommend removing the old turf completely, but a thorough tilling will suffice.

If you are starting a lawn on a new lot where the builder cut down everything in sight in order to facilitate construction of the house, chances are much of the topsoil on the lot has been removed or eroded. In many areas of the country the topsoil is deep enough that removal of the upper 4 or 5 inches of soil will not deplete the fertile soil on your lot. But in other areas, topsoil may be no more than 2 inches deep. In the South and in Texas, the layer of soil just under the topsoil may be hard clay or adobe soil. A tiller can break up hard, baked soils, but the first rain will compact the soil again. Unless you have access to an enormous quantity of compost or other organic matter that you can till into the soil to improve its structure, you will need to have topsoil hauled in to improve your lawn bed.

Unfortunately, there is no way to know the quality of the topsoil you buy until the truck arrives. Very likely, the topsoil will be full of rocks, sticks, and other debris, but this is virtually unavoidable. What's more important is the quality of the topsoil itself. Good topsoil is dark brown or black and crumbly. Top quality soil smells good, like the soil on a forest floor, rich in humus and decaying organic matter. The better the topsoil, the less fertilizer and other soil amendments will be required to build a rich lawn bed.

Till the bed before you add topsoil; then till it again after the topsoil has been spread and all debris removed from it. Grass roots may penetrate 24 to 30 inches deep and if the soil under your topsoil is hard and compacted, root growth and penetration will be poor no matter how high the quality of the topsoil you have added.

Till the lawn area thoroughly before attempting to plant. Inadequate soil preparation is the most frequent cause of failure with new lawns.

Till or rake in fertilizer and organic matter such as peat moss, leaf mold, rotted sawdust, or compost. Grade to a smooth, even surface.

After tilling, remove stones and other debris.

Fertilizing and liming

Fertilizer and lime should be tilled into the soil at the rates recommended by a soil test. Fertilizer supplies nutrients such as nitrogen, phosphorous, and potassium to the plants. These elements, and others that are contained in fertilizer, are necessary for plant growth. Lime reduces the acidity of soil. Depending on the total chemical composition of the soil, it may be acid or alkaline (sour or sweet, as our grandfathers used to call it). Some plants, such as azaleas and camellias, require acid soil. Soil acidity is measured on a scale called pH, with values assigned from 1 to 14. Neutral soil (neither acid nor alkaline) has a pH of 7.0. Below pH 7.0, the soil is said to be acid and

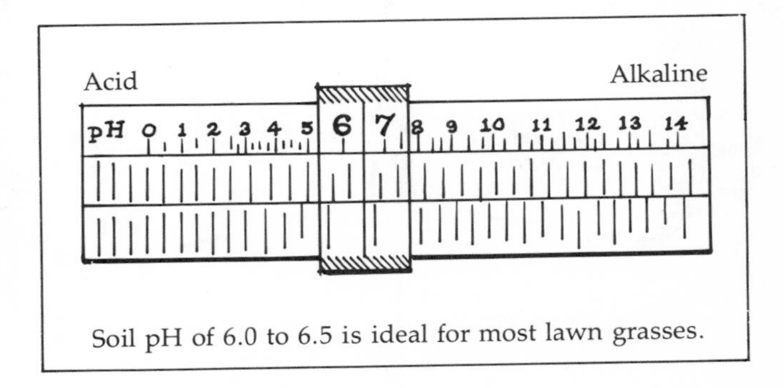

Soil pH of 6.0 to 6.5 is ideal for most lawn grasses.

above 7.0, alkaline. Most lawn grasses grow best in neutral soil. One exception is centipede grass which prefers a slightly acid soil with a pH of about 5.5. Generally speaking, soils in the North tend to be slightly alkaline and those in the South tend to be slightly acid. Nonetheless, add lime only if a soil test indicates a need for it. Lime may take up to 5 months to react with the soil, so test the soil and lime 3 to 5 months prior to planting.

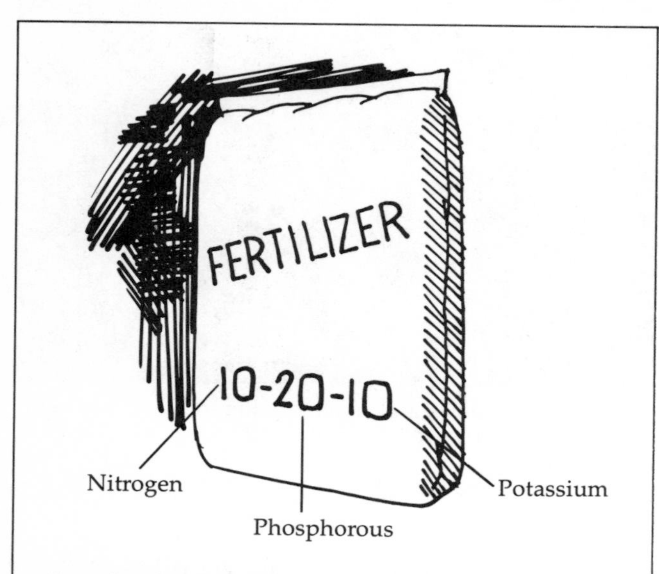

Complete fertilizer contains all three primary fertilizing elements: nitrogen, phosphorous, and potassium.

In addition to complete fertilizer, lawn grasses also need regular applications of nitrogen fertilizer.

If you do not have the soil tested, add fertilizer at the rate of 20 pounds per 1,000 square feet. To determine the size of your lawn area in square feet, multiply the length of the bed by its width. Thus, an area that is 100 feet long and 60 feet wide is 6,000 square feet. Apply complete fertilizer, that is, fertilizer which contains some measure of all three primary fertilizing elements: nitrogen, phosphorous, and potassium. The relative amounts of these elements will be indicated on the label by numbers such as 8–8–8. This means that the fertilizer contains 8 percent nitrogen, 8 percent phosphorous, and 8 percent potassium by weight. Lawn fertilizers are usually labeled as such, but it is always a good idea when purchasing fertilizer to tell the retailer exactly what you intend to fertilize.

Broadcast the fertilizer over the entire bed by hand or use a spreader. A spreader allows you to distribute the fertilizer evenly, but you can also do this by hand if you are careful. It is important to distribute fertilizer evenly to assure even growth. Till the fertilizer into the soil along with other soil amendments when you are preparing the planting bed. The preparatory tilling and fertilizing is best done 1 to 2 weeks prior to planting. This reduces the possibility of fertilizer burn on seeds or young plants.

Again, add lime only if a soil test recommends it.

Other soil amendments

If your soil is poor, it can be improved by adding organic matter. Compost, leaf mold, peat moss, pine straw, hay, sawdust, pine bark, or any other organic matter you can obtain in quantity will improve the soil by making it looser and more crumbly and, in the case of clay soil, by improving drainage. In coastal areas where the soil is very sandy, the addition of organic matter will improve the soil's ability to hold moisture. As organic matter decomposes, it also adds humus to the soil. Peat moss and pine bark, the most widely available soil amendments, can improve soil texture and moisture-holding capacity, but the amount of plant nutrient available in them is negligible.

You may also want to apply a preemergence herbicide to control weeds. Spread organic matter over the lawn bed and till it in. Don't worry about "overtilling"; there's no such thing. Till the soil and whatever soil amendments you have added until the mixture is uniformly fine and crumbly.

The finer the texture of your soil, the more easily plants can grow. Well-prepared soil permits water to drain rapidly and allows good air circulation. The extra effort expended at this stage of lawn building will assure success whereas half-hearted preparation of the lawn bed will result in disappointment.

Grading

The surface of the lawn bed must be even for two good reasons: to assure drainage of excess moisture and to permit even mowing. A simple

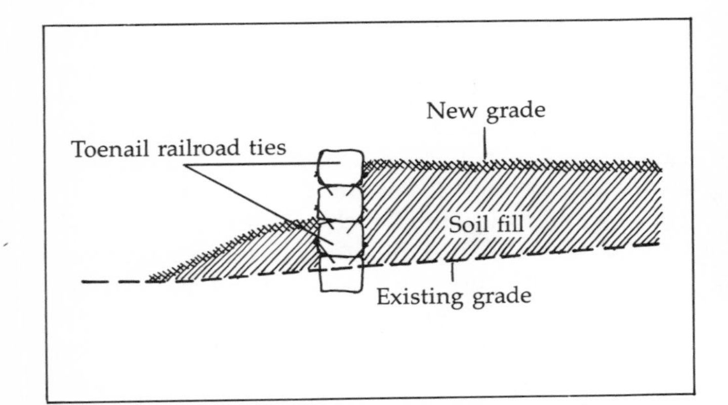

Altering the grade can increase the utility of the yard and at the same time add eye-pleasing lines to a static expanse of land.

Effective grade changes can transform unruly knolls and ridges into elegant and livable pockets in the home landscape.

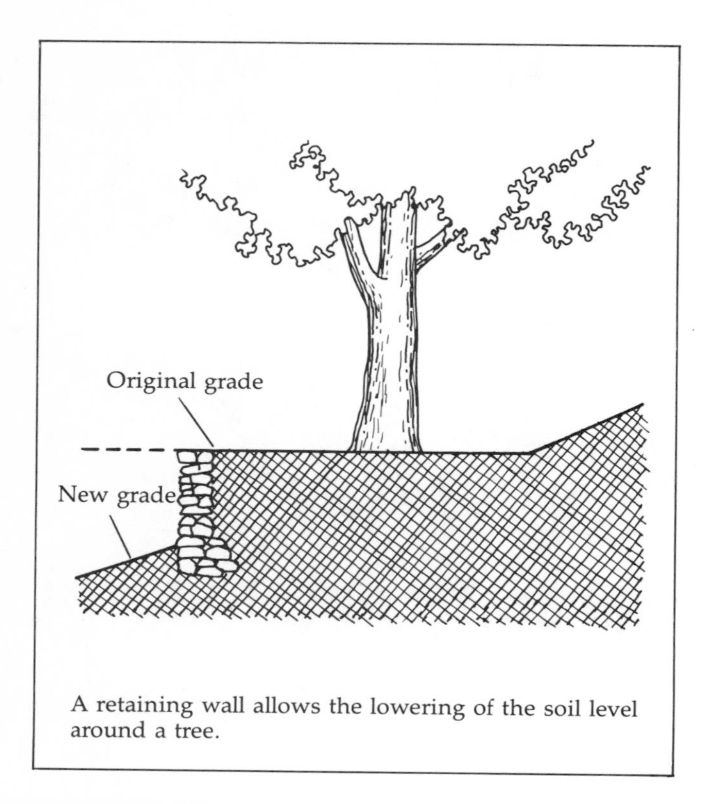

A retaining wall allows the lowering of the soil level around a tree.

garden rake is as good a device as any for grading the lawn. If you don't trust your eye to determine the evenness of the grade, drive a stake in the center of the bed and attach a string which will be long enough to reach the farthest point on the bed. With the string tied at soil level, you will be able to extend it to any point in the bed to see if you have leveled the bed evenly. Remove any clods, sticks, stones, or other debris which may still remain in the soil.

Making Grade Changes

If your lawn area slopes, you may want to terrace it to create an even play area. Terracing can also create an elegant effect, even in a small area. To make grade changes, you will need to build miniretaining walls. Common materials used for this purpose include railroad ties, stones, logs, and bricks. You will also need additional topsoil.

To determine the height of the retaining wall, drive a tall stake into the ground in the area where you think the retaining wall should be. Drive a second, shorter stake into the ground at the highest level to which you intend to raise the rest of the

Be sure to provide drainage outlets, or "weep holes," in the retaining wall. Otherwise, the soil behind the wall may collect excess moisture that drains from other areas of the yard.

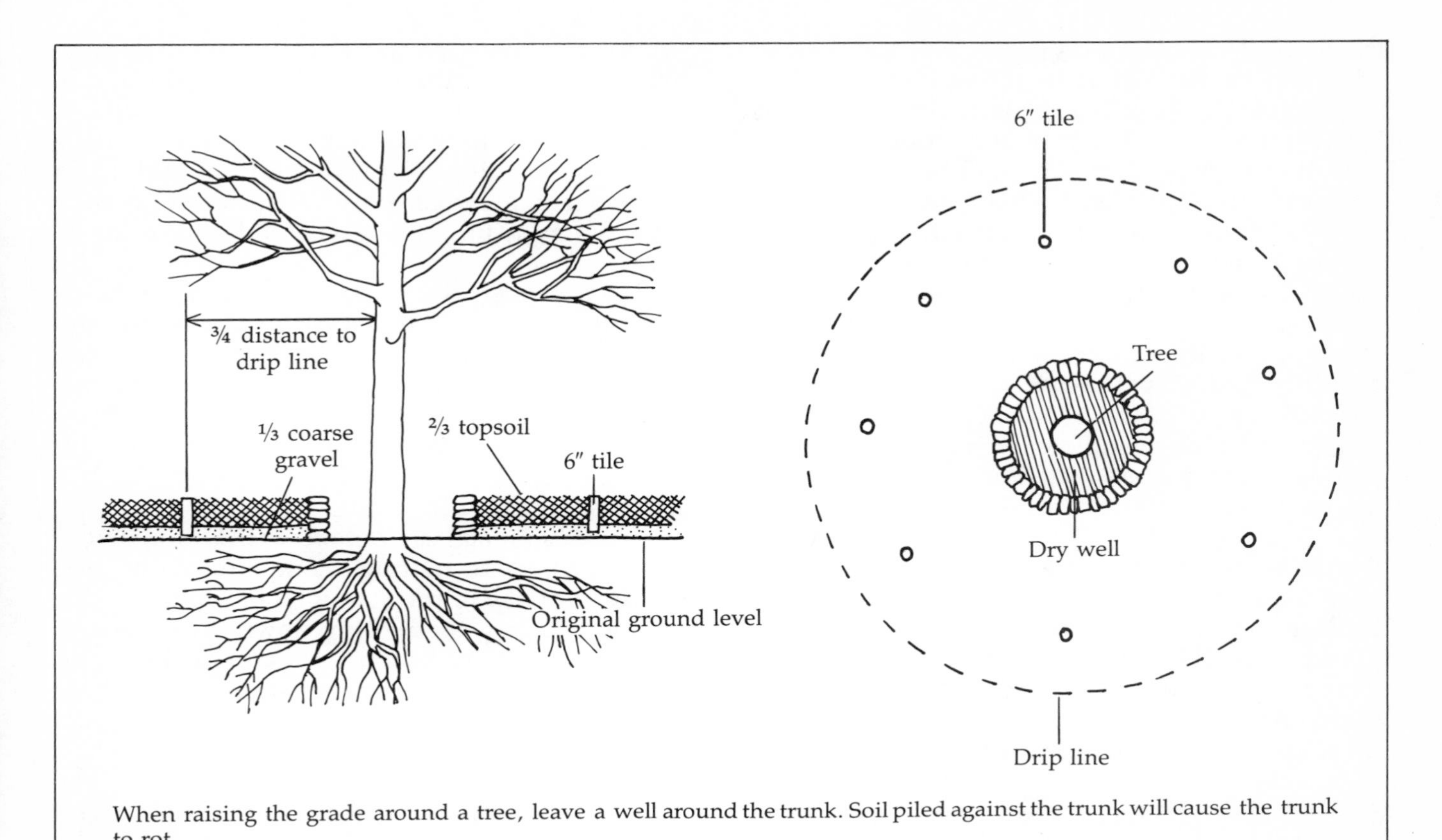

When raising the grade around a tree, leave a well around the trunk. Soil piled against the trunk will cause the trunk to rot.

bed. Attach a string at soil level to the shorter stake. Use a carpenter's level to determine the height at which the string should be attached to the tall stake at the lower end of the slope. This will give you a good idea of the level to which you must raise the grade at the lower end of the slope. For a more accurate reading, you may want to use a surveyor's transit.

If you build the retaining wall out of woody materials, be sure to treat the wood first with a nontoxic preservative such as copper napthenate. Otherwise, the part of the wooden wall that rests on or is buried in soil will decay. You may also buy pressure-treated wood that is decay-resistant.

Changing the grade of the soil around trees will require particular care. Lowering the grade may expose roots. Be certain to build the retaining wall far enough away from the tree so that damage from root pruning will not be severe. If you raise the soil level around a tree, build an inner protective wall around the trunk so that soil will not be piled against the trunk. This can cut off the supply of oxygen to the roots and will cause the trunk to decay and can kill the tree.

Whenever you use retaining walls, be sure to provide drainage by making "weep holes" in the base of the wall.

Planting the Lawn

Depending on the type of grass used, lawns are planted by seeding, sodding (laying sections of turf with grass already growing), sprigging (planting a small clump of grass with roots and top growth), or plugging (similar to sprigging, but using small squares of turf rather than clumps). Sprigging and plugging are methods which can be used only with types of grass that spread by *stolons* or *runners*, stems that grow on the surface of the soil or just below and then send up top growth.

Seeding

Broadcast seed by hand or use a spreader. In either case, even distribution of the seed is a must. The thicker you sow the seed, the thicker it will grow. Do not attempt to sow grass seed on a windy day. Even a slight breeze may hamper your ability to sow the seed evenly. If you use a mechanical spreader, distribute half the seed in an east to west direction; then distribute the other half in a north to south direction. The label on the bag of grass seed will tell you the proper setting to use on the spreader to sow the seed.

After you have distributed the seed, rake it in lightly. A lawn rake will be sufficient for this purpose; a garden rake may bury the seed too deep. Mulch the bed with a light material such as hay, sawdust, or damp peat moss and spread it very thinly. Don't attempt to cover the entire bed with a perfectly even layer of mulch or you may spread the mulch too thickly. A ¼-inch layer of mulch, distributed fairly evenly, will retard loss of surface moisture and prevent erosion without burying the seed too deep.

Once the bed is seeded and mulched, water the entire bed with a fine mist from the garden hose. Water by hand; a sprinkler may disturb the seed and cause some erosion. Until the grass is up, you should water the bed every day when there is no rain. If the germinating seed is allowed to dry out, it will die.

Watch the bed closely for the first few weeks to be sure the grass is growing evenly. Sprinkle seed on areas where no grass is coming up and scratch it in lightly. Avoid walking on the newly planted bed. If you must cross the bed frequently, lay a board across the bed to walk on. Reseed this area later, after the rest of the lawn is established.

Seeding on a slope

If you live in an area of sparse rainfall, seeding a lawn on a slope may not present problems. In most areas, however, the seed as well as the topsoil will be washed away with the first rain if precautions are not taken.

Prepare the bed in the usual way. If the soil surface is somewhat loose, rainwater will seep into the soil rather than wash down the slope. It is especially important to mulch the planted bed if it is on a slope. This alone may be adequate to hold the seed and soil in place. In addition to the fine mulch recommended for a flat seed bed, a light cover of hay or pine straw will hold everything in place.

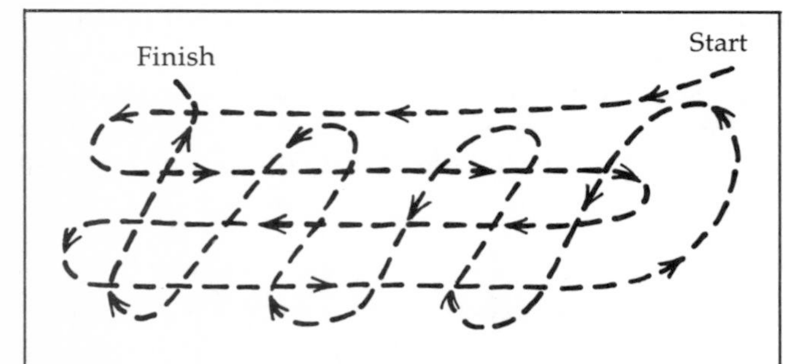

Divide the grass seed in half; then, distribute half in one direction and the other half at right angles to the first, as indicated in the diagram.

If, however, the slope is steep, or rainfall is torrential, it may be necessary to secure the seedbed more carefully. One method is to use coarsely woven strips of untreated burlap to cover the bed. These can be pegged down at the corners to hold them in place. As the grass grows and the lawn becomes established, the burlap will decompose in the soil.

Another material available to the homeowner is polypropylene netting. First, mulch the bed lightly with hay or pine straw; then, cover it with netting and peg the netting down. This type of netting has a ½- to 1-inch mesh and can be left on the lawn bed until the grass is fully established. Remove it before attempting to mow the new lawn, however.

Unless some precautions are taken, it will be futile to attempt to establish a lawn on a steep slope by seeding. You may save yourself a lot of time, money, topsoil, and aggravation by sodding the lawn. And, depending on the kind of grass you choose, it may be the only way.

Sodding

The fastest way to establish a lawn is to lay sections of turf with grass already established in them. This is also the most expensive method of installing a lawn. Some grasses, such as the Bermudas and zoysias, are best established in this manner. Lawn areas with a steep slope may erode before seeded or sprigged grasses can become established, especially in areas of high rainfall.

Prepare the lawn bed as for seeding. Grade the bed so that it slopes gently away from buildings or other places where water drainage could cause problems. Allow for settling; backfill around foundations of new homes may settle as much as 4 inches in the first 2 or 3 years.

Select high quality turfgrass and buy it from a reputable dealer. Good quality turf should be free of weeds, insects, and diseases.

Lay the sod as soon as possible after cutting, preferably the same day. Dampen the bed first, then lay the strips as close together as possible without causing wrinkles, overlapping, or air

After tilling and grading the lawn area, lay the strips of sod and butt them firmly together.

Roll the planted area with a water drum to iron out wrinkles and firm the grass roots against the soil.

pockets between the sod and the soil. See that all strips are butted firmly together.

On slopes start laying the strips at the lowest part of the incline. On particularly steep slopes it may be wise to peg the strips. Use three 6-inch pegs for each strip and drive one in near each end and one near the middle. Drive the pegs vertically, not perpendicularly, into the sod.

Roll the newly laid sod to eliminate air pockets under the strips and to firm the sod against the soil. Use a light 60- to 75-pound roller. Too much weight may cause the sod to creep. Roll each area—1,000 square feet—as it is laid.

Water the new lawn as soon as the entire area is sodded and rolled. A sprinkler system is sufficient for most of the lawn, but the corners, where the sprinkler may not reach, must be watered by hand. Water heavily until the sod is wet. If there is no rain, you should water the new lawn every day for the next 7 to 10 days. Do not allow the grass to wilt. Water in midafternoon when the sun is hottest. In 10 to 14 days, the roots should start to become established in the soil beneath the sod. After this, water only once a week. If rainfall is adequate, additional watering may not be necessary. Don't take chances with your new lawn; keep it well watered the first growing season. The deeper the roots penetrate, the less they will need to depend on artificial watering.

Sprigs and plugs

Spreading lawn grasses can be installed by planting small pieces of turf in a prepared lawn bed.

Sprigging is the most economical method of vegetative (plants as opposed to seeds) planting, but it is also the most tedious. Place a strip of sod rootside up, wash away the soil with a strong spray from the garden hose, and pull sprigs apart. Plant the sprigs 6 inches apart in a prepared bed,

Cut sections of sod into plugs 2 inches by 2 inches.

Plant the plugs at the desired interval and firm the soil around them. A series of perpendicular strings running the length and width of the lawn bed will help you set the plugs evenly.

leaving the grass blades above ground. A square yard of sod should furnish from 2,000 to 3,000 sprigs of grass, enough to cover 500 to 700 square feet. Dampen the planting bed before you set the sprigs and firm the soil around the roots. Common Bermuda can be planted by broadcasting sprigs over the prepared bed and raking them into the soil. Mulch the bed with hay or burlap to conserve moisture and to prevent erosion and compaction. A light mulch of hay, no more than ½ inch thick, will suffice.

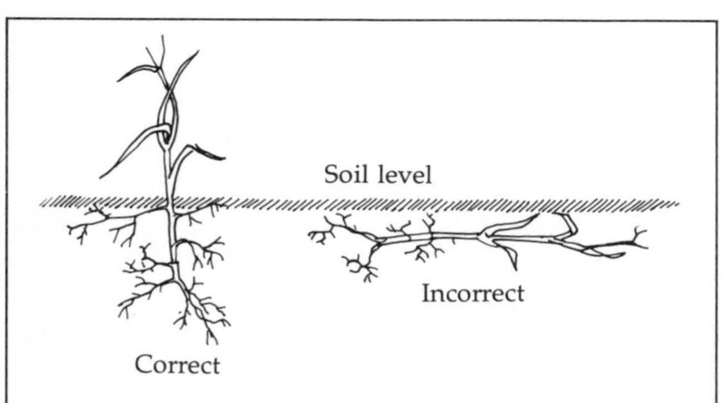

Plant sprigs upright and firm soil around the roots. Do not cover them; only common Bermuda can be grown by raking the sprigs into the soil.

Plugging is easier and faster than sprigging and much less expensive than sodding. A square yard of sod will furnish 324 (2-inch) plugs. This is enough to cover 324 square feet of bed if the plugs are planted 12 inches apart. For faster cover, plant this number of plugs 6 inches apart to cover 81-square feet of area. Mulch between the plugs with burlap or hay, especially on slopes.

The time required for complete coverage can be shortened considerably with judicious watering and fertilizing. Keep the soil continuously moist but not saturated. Give the grass a very light application of nitrogen fertilizer every 2 weeks.

Ammonium nitrate and ammonium sulfate are both good fertilizers for this purpose and are applied at the rate of about ½ pound per 1,000 square feet. Keep the surface absolutely free of weeds and other grasses.

To further encourage the grass to spread more rapidly, begin mowing as soon as the new shoots are about 3 inches high. Adjust the mower to cut 2 inches high.

Edgings for Planting Beds

To prevent the spread of grasses into flower beds and to facilitate mowing along beds, you should provide an edge. Materials commonly used for edging are brick, concrete, metal, plastic, and wood. A trim edge between planting beds and lawn is both attractive and practical.

Because spreading grasses such as zoysia or the Bermudas send out underground runners, the edging must be deep enough to provide an effective barrier. Select a material which will be at least 8 to 10 inches deep and nearly as wide. Redwood, cedar, or pressure-treated pine are good materials for straight edges. Railroad ties are also useful for this purpose. Remember to treat any woody material with a wood preservative such as copper napthenate. Otherwise the wood will decay rapidly.

For edgings that curve, poured concrete or bricks can provide a suitable and attractive edging.

Chemical herbicides are also used to provide edgings. Though the buffer zone created in this way has no architectural value, it does effectively prevent the encroachment of lawn grasses on flower beds and vice versa.

An edging that separates the lawn from planting beds facilitates maintenance of both. Commonly used edging materials include logs, railroad ties, brick, and concrete.

Rejuvenating an Old Lawn

If a lawn is not properly cared for, it will soon deteriorate. You may inherit a neglected lawn if you buy property from a disinterested homeowner or if the property has been vacant for a year or more. Or if your first attempt to build a lawn failed, you will have to try again.

A typically poor lawn has thin turf, a lot of bare spots, dead or dying grass, and an army of weeds. The chief causes of lawn deterioration are poor drainage, careless selection of grass, improper mowing, inadequate insect and disease control, improper fertilization and liming, and too much shade. Probably the greatest cause of failure with lawns, however, is inadequate preparation of the soil when the lawn was first constructed. More than likely, no soil test was performed and it was therefore impossible to know exactly how much fertilizer to add or if lime was needed to adjust soil acidity.

If the lawn has deteriorated too far—spotted with bare patches and rampant with weeds—you will have to reconstruct it completely. As a general guideline, if less than half the lawn consists of desirable grasses, reconstruction will be necessary. Till the lawn area completely to break up the old turf, then add topsoil, fertilizer, organic matter, or other soil amendments necessary to obtain a rich, loose bed on which to grow a healthy turf. (See Chapters One and Two.)

Often enough the existing lawn can be renovated by reworking the deteriorated areas.

First, get rid of all leaves and other surface debris that may be preventing the lawn from receiving adequate sunlight and moisture. Next, mow the lawn as closely as possible and rake the clippings with a garden rake to remove not only the fresh clippings but also any buildup of old clippings and debris which may have settled into the soil. This process, which should be performed routinely at least once a year, is called *dethatching*. A vigorous raking with a firm-toothed rake also loosens the surface to create a rough seed bed.

Level any areas where depressions may have formed by adding topsoil. In areas where winters are severe, alternate freezing and thawing may cause frost heaves and ridges. It may be necessary to dig and turn the soil thoroughly in selected areas of the lawn to level frost heaves and other humps.

Be sure to get as much of the root system of weedy plants as possible; otherwise, you will be digging up the same weeds in a few weeks or months. Selective herbicides may be useful for eliminating crabgrass and other lawn weeds. Broadleaf weeds can be controlled with 2,4-D and narrowleaf weeds with DSMA. Such herbicides are most effective early in the season when weeds are just beginning to emerge. Avoid using 2,4-D or DSMA on St. Augustine and centipede lawns as they may damage the grass.

To fertilize and lime effectively, it is best to collect a pint of your soil to be analyzed by the soil testing laboratory of your state agricultural extension service. Only with such an analysis can you be absolutely certain of how much fertilizer and lime, if any, you should add to the soil. It is as important to test the soil in an old lawn as in a new one; if you have to rebuild the lawn, a soil test will help take the guesswork out of diagnosing your lawn problems. If you don't have the soil tested, don't apply lime. A safe fertilizer application consists of about 20 pounds of complete fertilizer, such as 8–8–8 or 10–6–4, per 1,000 square feet of lawn area. Dampen the area before applying fertilizer; then rake the fertilizer into the soil surface. Do not overfertilize; this can cause root damage to the tiny seedling plants as they begin to grow. For spot seeding apply ½ cup of fertilizer to an area of 1 square yard (3 feet × 3 feet). It may be wise to use dehydrated manure or cottonseed meal fertilizer for very small areas since these reduce the danger of fertilizer burn. After applying fertilizer, water the area again.

Be certain to purchase the type and variety of grass that matches the existing lawn grass. To match a coarse leaf grass such as St. Augustine with a fine leaf, slow-growing variety of centipede can cause a patchy effect. Color variation from variety to variety is great enough to also merit attention.

Since not all grass is propagated from seed, you may need to plant sprigs, plugs, or sections of turf (called sod). Consult the chart *Selecting Lawn Grasses* at the end of Chapter One to determine the proper planting method for the type of grass you have. The retailer from whom you buy seed or turf will also be able to advise you. Bring a small clump of your lawn grass with you for identification.

To level humps and frost heaves, chop out strips of mounded sod and use the excess soil to fill in depressions. Replace the sod and water the doctored area thoroughly.

If you purchase seed, sprinkle the seed evenly over the prepared area and scratch it into the soil with a garden rake. Firm the soil with your hand if the area is small. For larger areas, firm the soil with a board or lawn roller (available from rental agencies, especially those featuring lawn and garden equipment).

Water the planted area with a fine mist from the garden hose. The finer the mist, the less chance of disturbing the soil and the seeds. Seeded areas on slopes should be mulched with a light cover (¼ to ½ inch) of hay or pine straw. Keep the area well watered until the grass is established and growing.

If you plant sprigs or plugs, prepare the planting areas as for seeding. Dig small furrows and place the sprigs and plugs 6 to 12 inches apart. Firm the soil around them and water the planted area with a fine mist.

If you lay sod, the level of the prepared bed should be about ½ inch lower than the surrounding soil. Cut the sod to fit snugly in place and be sure the sod is butted tightly against the adjoining sod strips. Sod cut too small will leave a visible margin and those cut too large will buckle and wrinkle. Dampen the prepared bed before laying the sod. Firm the sod against the soil with a board or, in large areas, with a lawn roller. After the sod is in place and wrinkles have been smoothed, water the planted area thoroughly. Keep the area watered for at least 2 weeks. Newly sodded areas should be watered every day until the grass is well rooted—for about 2 or 3 weeks.

Avoid walking on newly planted areas, if possible, until the grass is established and growing well.

To renovate small areas of the lawn, turn the soil with a spade.

Next, break up the clods, rake the bed smooth, and replant.

Routine Care of the Lawn

The key to a beautiful, well-kept lawn is proper maintenance. With good care, you can keep your lawn attractive, easing the transition between the verdant new growth of spring and the stresses of summer. Feeding, watering, mowing, weeding, and controlling insects and diseases are important factors for all lawns. Neglect only one and the result can be a thin, unsightly lawn.

Mowing

Improper mowing is responsible for the demise of many lawns. Mow the grass often enough so that you remove only about a third of the leaf blade at any one clipping. Grass manufactures food in the leaf blades. When too much of the blade is removed, the entire plant suffers.

Most lawns should be mowed weekly. Collect the clippings; they are useful as mulch material for flower beds and vegetable gardens. They also break down into usable compost in 2 to 4 weeks.

Another reason for removing clippings after mowing is that the clippings, when left on the lawn, eventually form a layer of thatch on the soil surface. This thatch hampers the penetration of water and air into the soil and if not removed regularly, can ultimately destroy large areas of the lawn. Zoysiagrasses are especially prone to this problem.

Use a mower with a sharp blade set at the

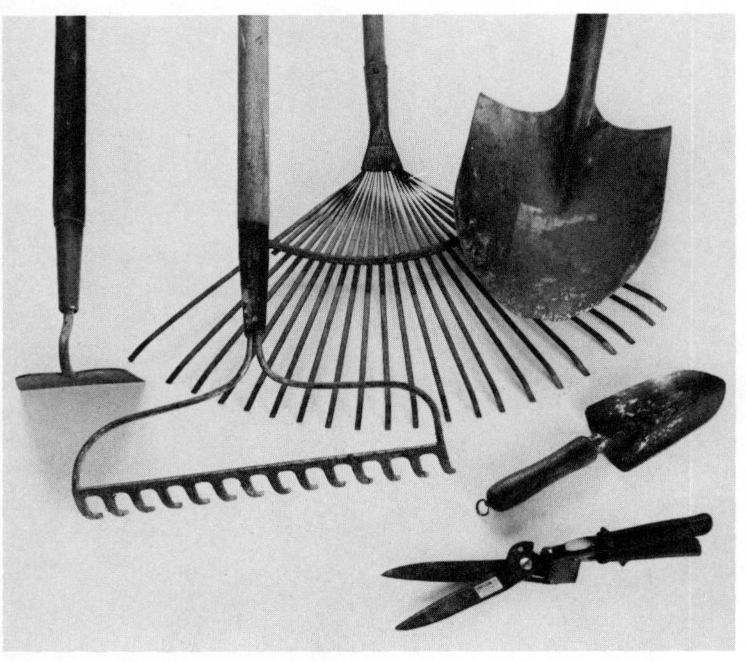

Basic hand tools for lawn care include (clockwise from left): hoe, garden rake, lawn rake, spade, trowel, and grass shears.

correct mowing height. For cool-season grasses this is about 2 inches. Close mowing, especially during hot weather, greatly weakens all cool-season grasses, whether bluegrass, fescue, or bent.

Recommended mowing heights vary somewhat with lawn grasses. St. Augustine is normally cut about 3 inches high, while common Bermuda, zoysia, and centipede are cut at about 1½ inches.

During the hottest summer months grasses will benefit if the mower blade is raised as much as ½ inch. This allows for more shading of the root system, resulting in less weed seed germination and better conservation of soil moisture.

Vacation time during the summer may present a problem with mowing. If you cannot find someone to cut the grass while you are away, return it to normal mowing height gradually. This can be done by cutting in a series of progressively lower mowings a few days apart.

A power mower is a necessary piece of equipment for maintaining an attractive lawn. But it can also cause trouble, even fatal injury, when used in a careless manner or in the presence of pets and children. Before starting to mow, pick up any toys, sticks, stones, pieces of wire, or other loose objects that could become deadly missiles when struck by the whirling blade of a mower.

Keep the mower in good mechanical condition through proper maintenance. A blade that is out of balance will cause vibration and excessive wear. Operate the mower only fast enough to get a good, clean cut; extremely high blade speeds are dangerous.

Mow across slopes rather than up and down. A slip could mean the loss of a foot. If the mower becomes clogged, stop the engine and disconnect the sparkplug wire before attempting to do any work beneath the mower. Do not fill the gas tank while the engine is hot. Check the oil and gas levels before starting the engine each time you use the mower.

Use hand clippers or a mechanical edger to trim grass around trees and along fences, buildings, and other places where the mower cannot cut.

Watering

In most areas of the country, rainfall is sufficient to keep the lawn adequately watered. During the dry months, however, and in areas of sparse rainfall, some irrigation will be necessary.

Frequency of watering depends not only on the frequency and amount of rainfall, it also depends on soil type and depth, the age of the lawn (young grass needs more water), root competition from other plants, and the efficiency of your watering system.

Soils vary a great deal in their moisture-retaining ability. Sandy soils drain very rapidly,

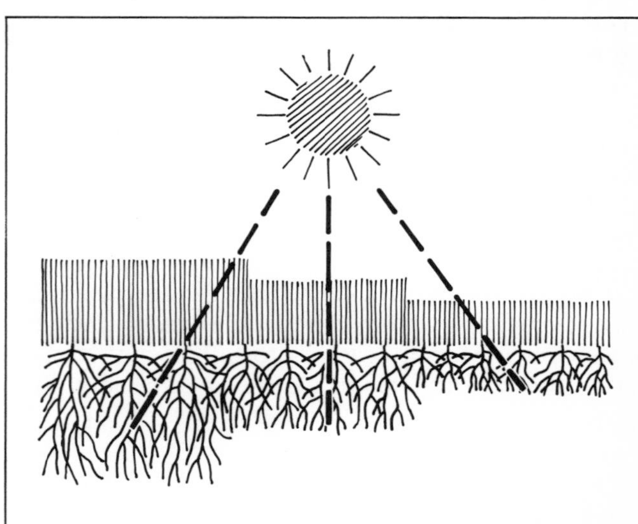

Grass blades that are cut at the correct height shade grass roots from midsummer heat, thereby encouraging deeper, sturdier roots.

Mow the lawn weekly so that you never need remove too much of the blades at one time.

A riding mower is the most versatile grass-cutting tool for large areas.

requiring the most frequent watering. Clay soils hamper water penetration, often causing water to run off the surface, particularly on sloping land, rather than to drain through the soil. Loamy soils permit good drainage without allowing moisture to move so rapidly through the soil that grass roots cannot benefit from it. Even more important than the type of top soil is the subsoil beneath the top layer. A layer of clay, rock, or other impervious material may cause water to back up and clog grass roots. To determine the type of soil you have, dig with a spade to a depth of 1 to 2 feet. Grass roots, especially in their first years of growth, can penetrate to a depth of 24 to 30 inches.

Competition from other plants also affects the amount of moisture available to grass roots in your lawn. Trees, shrubs, herbaceous ornamentals, and weeds all compete with your grass for moisture and nutrients. Judicious weed control, therefore, will affect your watering schedule.

Sprinkler systems vary a great deal in their ability to distribute water. In general, most lawn sprinkler systems deliver 4 to 6 gallons of water a minute. To distribute 1 inch of water over an area of 1,000 square feet, you would need to run the

This mechanical edger is a welcome alternative to manual clipping shears for cutting areas where conventional mowers cannot easily maneuver.

sprinkler for 2 to 2½ hours. Few sprinklers distribute water evenly, however.

To assess the evenness of your system's distribution, set containers around the lawn within the range of the sprinkler and run the sprinkler for 2 hours. This will not only demonstrate how much water is being distributed at various distances from the sprinkler, it will also let you know where to place the sprinkler head for it to water your lawn as effectively as possible.

The first symptoms of the need for water are wilting, dull color, and loss of resiliency in the lawn. A well-watered lawn is spongy. If, after walking across the lawn, you can see your footprints, it's time to water.

Water the lawn deeply when you do water. In loamy soil, run the sprinkler for 3 to 4 hours, depending on the type and depth of soil. A deep watering once a week is far more beneficial than light, daily watering. Light watering does not penetrate below the upper 2 or 3 inches of the soil, thereby encouraging roots to stay near the surface where moisture is available. Deep watering encourages roots to grow deep. Since there is more natural moisture in the subsoil than near the surface, roots encouraged to penetrate deeply will, in time, become more self-sufficient, less dependent on manual watering.

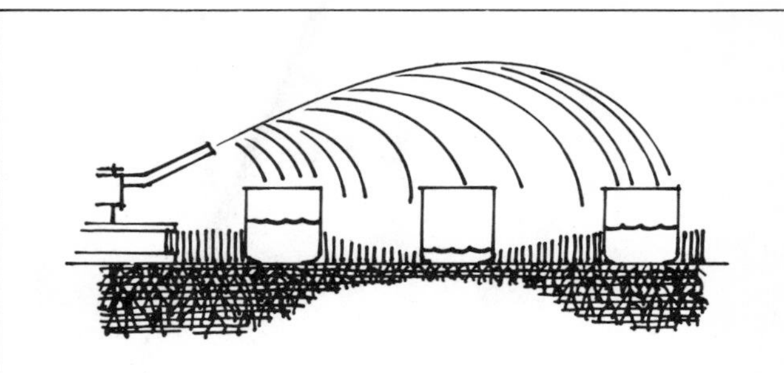

Set containers at various intervals from the sprinkler to measure the sprinkler's delivery capacity. Note that the areas receiving the most water develop the best grass roots.

This siamese shutoff valve with individual controls for each hose doubles the area you can water at one time.

Sandy soils are exceptional; since water drains through them rapidly, light, frequent watering is more beneficial. Water sandy soil twice or three times a week, depending on rainfall.

Until you are able to recognize the symptoms of water stress in your lawn, the best thing for you to do is check the soil with a trowel or shovel before watering. Don't water soil that is wet, but don't let it become completely dry either.

The best times to water are early morning and later afternoon. Water applied at midday is lost through evaporation (on hot days) and water left to stand on grass at night encourages the spread of fungus diseases.

Fertilizing

A number of commercial lawn fertilizers are available to the homeowner. Fertilizers provide nutrients to plants, helping to make vigorous, healthy growth.

The principal fertilizing elements are nitrogen, phosphorous, and potassium. So important to plant growth are these elements that any fertilizer containing all three is called a "complete fertilizer." In addition to nitrogen, phosphorous, and potassium, most fertilizers also contain calcium, magnesium, boron, zinc, and a number of other minor fertilizing elements called trace elements.

Fertilizers are classified as organic or chemical. Those fertilizers derived from decayed animal or vegetable matter, such as manures and cottonseed meal, are called organic fertilizers. Those produced by chemical extraction or manufacture are called chemical fertilizers. Because of the low cost of chemical manufacture compared to the availability of organic fertilizers, chemical fertilizers are generally less expensive than organic fertilizers.

The best fertilizers are those that release plant nutrients slowly and evenly over a long period of time. These fertilizers are also the most expensive. Highly soluble fertilizers not only produce rapid, erratic growth that may be weak, but these fertilizers can also burn plant roots when used without caution. Furthermore, highly soluble fertilizers may wash (leach) through the soil more rapidly than the plants can assimilate and use the nutrients they contain. This is true especially of chemical fertilizers. Manure, unless you buy packaged manure, should always be composted before being applied to the lawn or garden.

Commercial fertilizers are often sold according to their use. Rose food, azalea-camellia food, or lawn and turf food are examples.

Fertilizers are also labeled according to their chemical analysis, such as 8–8–8 or 10–10–10. These numbers, which are printed on the label, refer to the relative amounts of nitrogen, phosphorous, and potassium contained in the fertilizer; 8–8–8 contains, by weight, 8 percent nitrogen, 8 percent phosphorous, and 8 percent potassium.

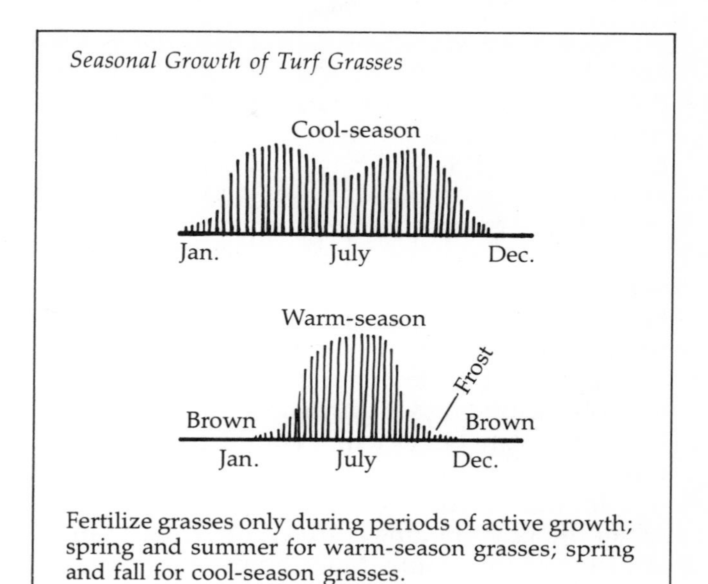

Fertilize grasses only during periods of active growth; spring and summer for warm-season grasses; spring and fall for cool-season grasses.

Most lawn grasses should be fertilized early in the growing season at the rate of 20 pounds of complete fertilizer per 1,000 square feet. Depending on the length of the growing season in your area and the type of grass you have, you will need to make 1 to 3 subsequent applications of nitrogen fertilizer at 2-month intervals. This schedule may vary considerably depending on the type of grass, the climate, and the fertilizer used. Centipede and carpetgrasses, for instance, require less fertilizer than Bermudas or fescues.

Unfertilized thin turf permits weeds to grow without competition.

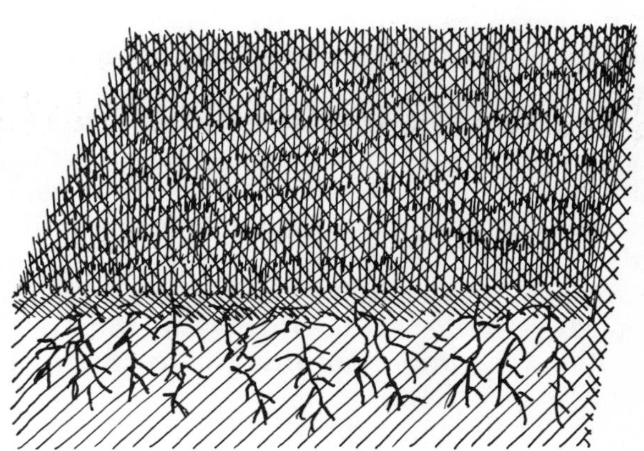

Fertilizer promotes thicker turf by helping desirable plants develop vigorous roots capable of crowding out weeds.

Warm-season grasses, which make their growth between spring and fall, should be fertilized at 2-month intervals beginning in early spring. Cool-season grasses should be fertilized in early spring, late spring, and early fall. Withhold fertilizer during the hot summer months when these grasses are less active.

In most of the South apply fertilizer to warm-season grasses in March, June, and August. Fertilize cool-season grasses at 2-month intervals from September to May, but withhold fertilizer during the hot summer months. Fertilizer applied to cool-season grasses during the summer will do little for the grass and will, in fact, benefit only the weeds.

In the North, fertilize cool season grasses when the grass begins to green up, then again in late May or early June. Make a final application at the beginning of September.

In the western coastal regions, follow the southern schedule. In the Midwest and in the mountainous regions of the West, follow the northern schedule if your area is covered with snow during the winter.

For specific rates of application you should consult your county agricultural extension agent whose telephone number you will find listed under the county government offices. Most will recommend between 15 and 25 pounds of fertilizer per 1,000 square feet. This may vary with soil type, the length of the growing season, the amount of annual rainfall, the type of grass, and the type of fertilizer used.

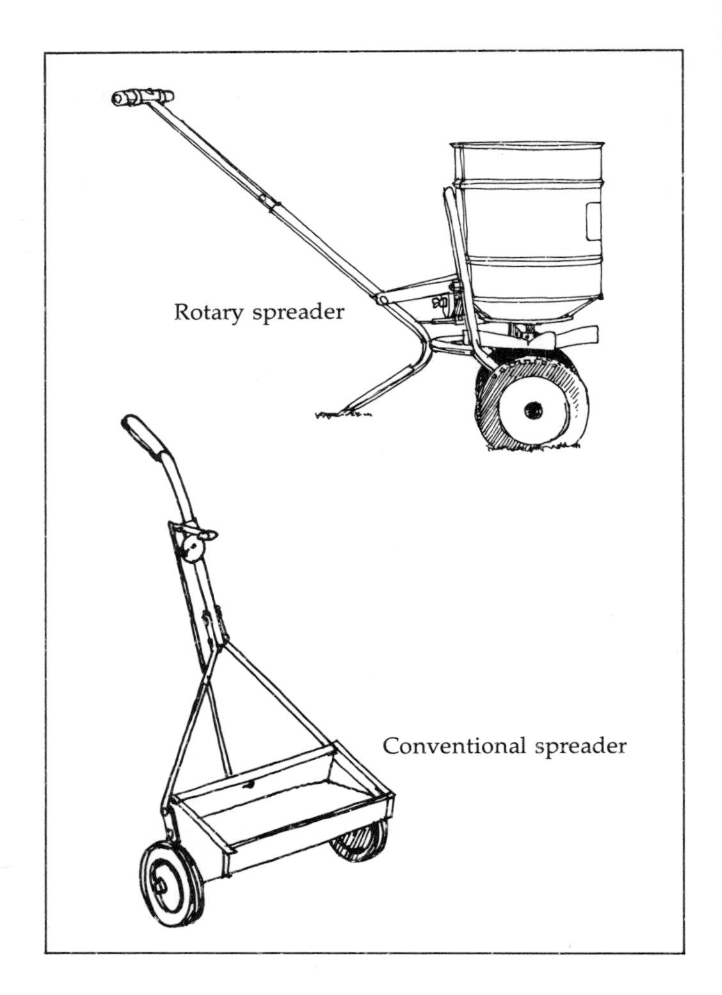

Applying fertilizer

You can broadcast (scatter) fertilizer by hand or in a small mechanical spreader. Spreaders are available at garden supply centers and rental agencies.

If you broadcast by hand, wear disposable household gloves or use a tin can to scoop chemical fertilizers. Prolonged contact of chemical fertilizers with bare skin may cause something a little rougher than dishpan hands. Organic fertilizers are less irritating and easier to handle. Regardless of the fertilizer or the method of distribution, the important thing is to spread it as evenly as possible.

The best time to apply fertilizer is the first dry day after a rain; the soil is moist, but the leaves of the grass are not wet. Don't wait for a rain if the lawn needs fertilizer. Spread the fertilizer evenly; then brush the grass with the back of a garden rake to shift the fertilizer down to the soil. Water the entire lawn thoroughly. Depending on the capacity of your sprinkler and the dryness of the soil, a *thorough* watering means from 2 to 4 hours. This washes the remainder of the fertilizer off the leaves and down into the soil. It is important to wash the fertilizer off the leaves; if left to dry on the leaves, the fertilizer could burn them.

Store fertilizers and other garden chemicals in a safe, dry place, out of the reach of children and pets.

Fertilizing grass under trees

Grass growing under established trees or near shrubs will need extra nitrogen fertilizer to help it overcome the problem of root competition. Since many tree roots are within the upper 6 to 12 inches of soil, the additional fertilizer will stimulate growth of the tree as well as that of the grass.

When fertilizing these areas, put on twice the amount of fertilizer recommended for the open lawn. Apply the fertilizer to an area approximately 3 feet from the trunk of the tree to at least 3 feet beyond the spread of the branches.

If additional fertilizer is not used on turf around an established tree, the tree will eventually win out. Roots of grasses do not live as long as tree roots and cannot compete satisfactorily over a long period of time. The turf then shows symptoms of decline by becoming less resistant to traffic, drought, insects, and diseases. The additional fertilizer will help the turf resist these problems.

Treating iron deficiency

If the lawn appears yellow even after it has been fertilized and watered regularly, your soil may be deficient in iron, another essential plant nutrient. This can be corrected with either iron chelate or ferrous sulfate. Dissolve either of these in water according to the directions on the label and apply recommended dosage to affected areas.

Liming to adjust soil acidity

Lawns in much of the country may require lime every 3 to 4 years to maintain the correct level of soil acidity. The best time to apply lime is in late fall or winter if the ground does not freeze for the entire winter. This allows time for the lime to work its way into the soil during periods of heavy precipitation and freezing and thawing.

Most lawn grasses grow best in soil that is slightly acid (pH 6.5), but perform poorly under highly acid conditions. On a scale of 0 to 14, a soil pH level of 7.0 is considered neutral, neither acid or alkaline. Below pH 7.0 the soil is said to be acid; above pH 7.0 the soil is alkaline.

The amount of lime needed to raise the pH level of the soil is determined by the present pH level, the texture and type of soil, and the amount of organic matter in it. Light soils require less lime than heavy soils; those low in organic matter require less than highly organic soils. The approximate amounts of ground limestone required to raise the soil reaction one pH unit are as follows:

Soil Type	*Lbs. per 1,000 sq. ft.*
Light, sandy	35
Sandy loam	45
Loam	70
Silt, clay loam	80

Two types of lime are generally recommended for use by homeowners: calcitic and dolomitic limestone. Both also supply calcium in addition to adjusting soil pH. Dolomitic limestone contains magnesium as well.

Hydrated lime reacts much faster than ground limestone, but it is not as long lasting. In either case, a spreader distributes the lime more evenly than broadcasting by hand.

Only a soil test can tell you for certain if your soil pH needs to be altered. Collect a pint of soil from various sections of the lawn and send it to the office of the county agricultural extension agent. He will forward it to a soil testing laboratory where it will be analyzed. Such a test will also indicate fertilizer deficiencies and make precise fertilizer recommendations. You may call the county agent's office (listed in most directories under county government) for instructions on sending the soil sample to be tested.

Weed Control in Lawns

A poor lawn is usually the cause rather than the result of weeds. Not many weeds can even get a start in a lawn that has a dense, healthy sod.

If a lawn grass is adapted to the area where it is used, and if proper feeding, watering, mowing, and insect and disease controls are followed, weed problems will be far easier to control. When any of these practices are ignored, the grass is weakened and weeds can be expected to invade the lawn.

When weeds are a problem, either chemical control (selective herbicides) or mechanical control (hand weeding and mowing) can be effective. If the infestation is light, hand weeding or mowing is perhaps the most practical solution. Regular, frequent mowing will eliminate many weeds. In some cases, however, the best solution is to use a herbicide.

The objective of weed control in established lawns is to kill the weeds while doing as little damage as possible to the desirable lawn grass. To meet these objectives, selective herbicides are used.

It is not necessary for the gardener to know the exact identity of each weed he is trying to kill. But he should know how to distinguish between grassy and broadleaf weeds because they require different types of herbicides.

The grassy weeds include nutgrass, crabgrass, Johnsongrass, annual bluegrass, goosegrass, and dallisgrass. Broadleaf weeds make up the larger group of weeds that invade lawns. These include such familiar kinds as dandelion,

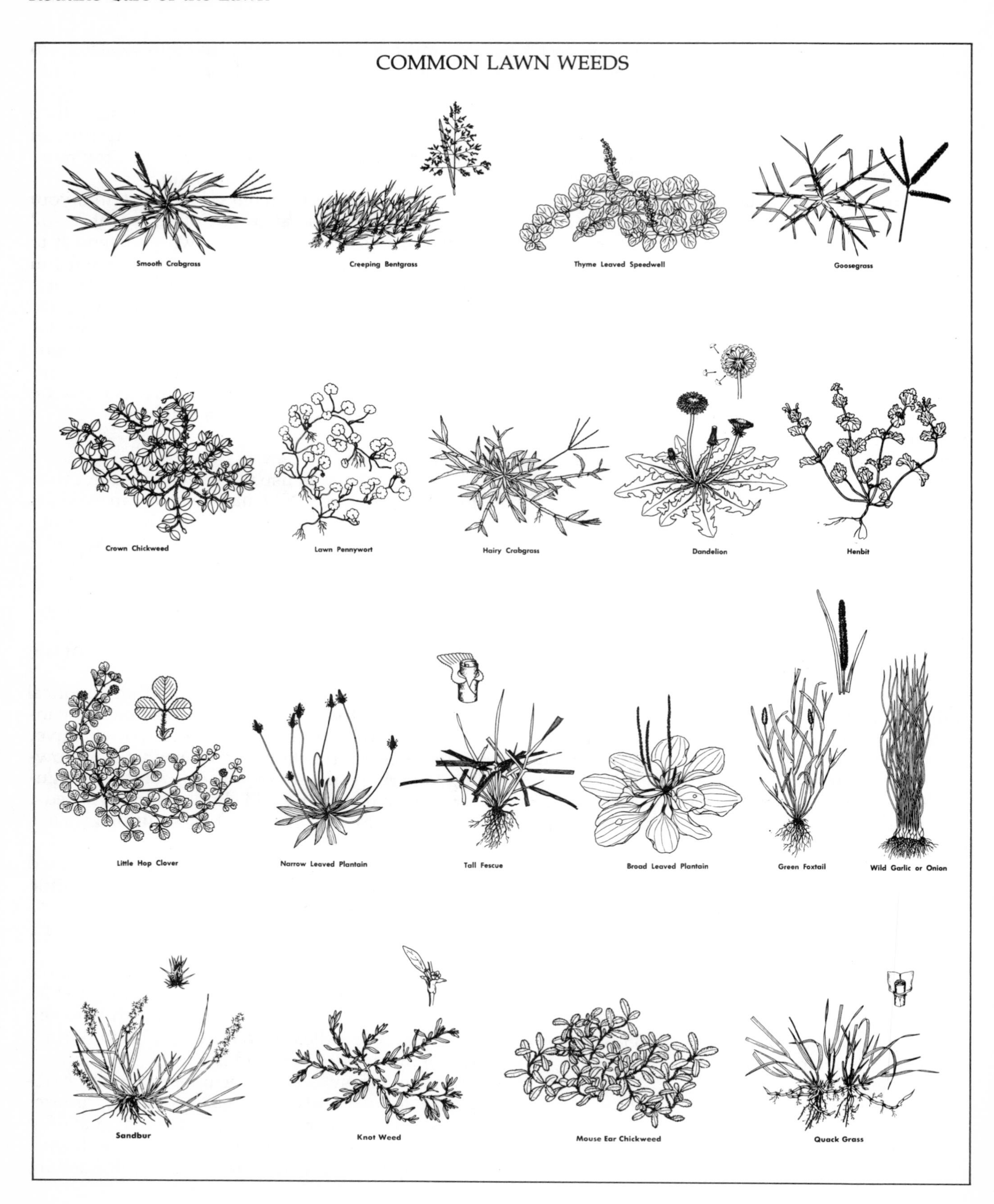
COMMON LAWN WEEDS
Smooth Crabgrass
Creeping Bentgrass
Thyme Leaved Speedwell
Goosegrass
Crown Chickweed
Lawn Pennywort
Hairy Crabgrass
Dandelion
Henbit
Little Hop Clover
Narrow Leaved Plantain
Tall Fescue
Broad Leaved Plantain
Green Foxtail
Wild Garlic or Onion
Sandbur
Knot Weed
Mouse Ear Chickweed
Quack Grass

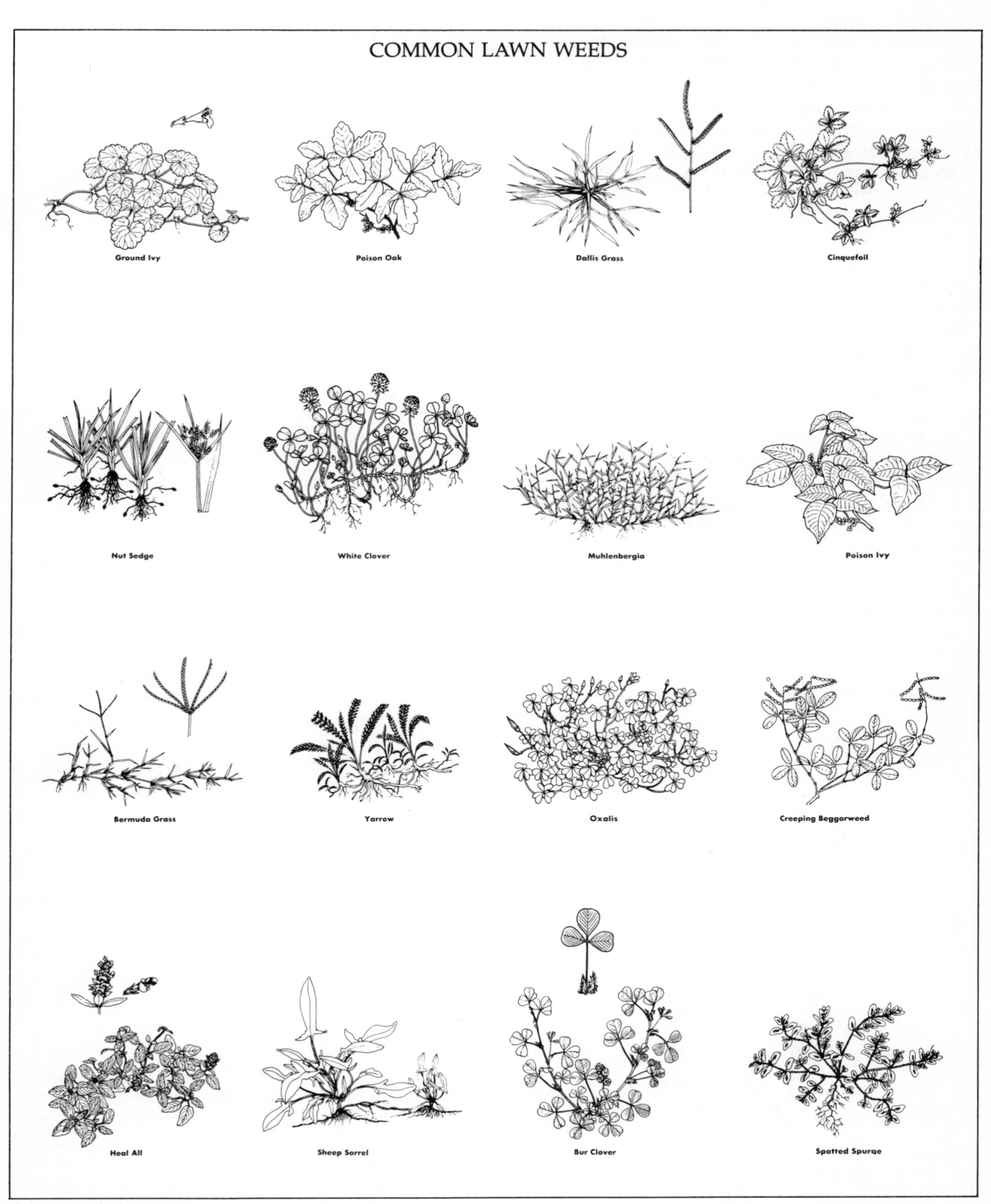

Courtesy of Amchem

chickweed, henbit, plantain, buckhorn, and spurge. These weeds can be controlled with materials containing either silvex or the amine form of 2,4-*D*. (Caution: Both of these herbicides will injure many ornamentals and crop plants if the spray gets on the foliage.) Spray to wet the leaves of weeds when no rain is expected for 6 to 8 hours. Repeat treatment in 7 to 10 days to control hard-to-kill weeds. Do not apply to St. Augustine grass; injury may also occur on centipede.

Herbicides may be purchased in either powder, granulated, or liquid forms and in different concentrations. Information on rates, methods of application, precautions, and limitations of any given product is listed on the manufacturer's label. Follow these directions explicitly.

The effectiveness of herbicides is influenced by many factors. Generally, they are more effective on young, rapidly growing plants. They are usually less effective against weeds at temperatures below 60° F. and above 85° F.

Herbicides may be applied by almost any means that gets them in contact with the weed. The compressed-air sprayer and the hose-attachment sprayer are widely used for applying liquids, wettable powders, and emulsifiable concentrates. Solid-type herbicides, in powder or granulated forms, may be applied with a fertilizer spreader.

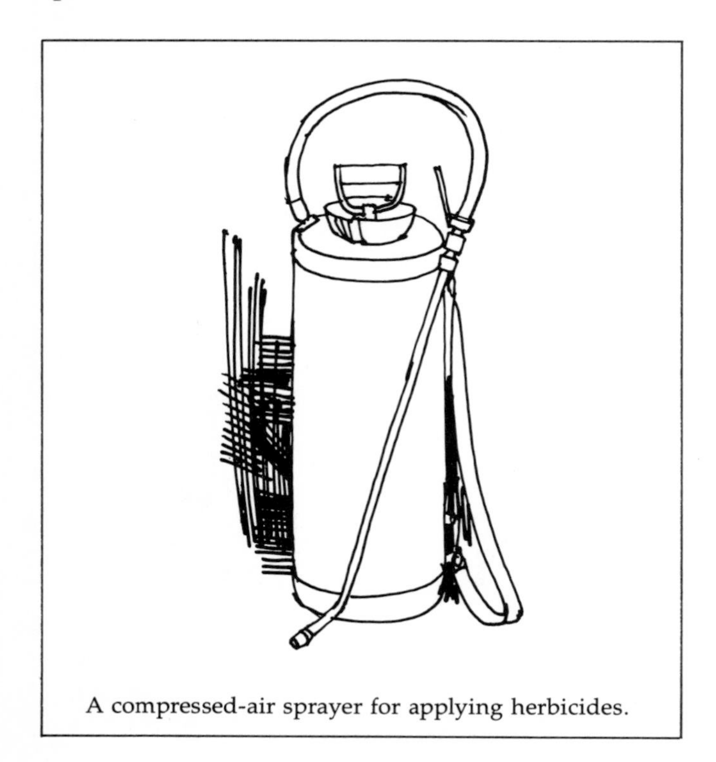

A compressed-air sprayer for applying herbicides.

Fertilizer-herbicide combinations

Many fertilizer-herbicide mixtures are available commercially. Combining the two makes application somewhat more convenient, reducing two operations to one. The greatest problem with these combinations is that applications of the two agents are not necessarily meant to coincide. For example, a fertilizer containing a preemergence crabgrass killer might be applied in the fall when, in fact, the crabgrass herbicide should be applied in the spring. Or combination fertilizer and broadleaf weed herbicides are often applied when no broadleaf weeds are present in the lawn. A further complication arises when such a combination is used in midsummer to control weeds in cool-season grasses, a period when cool-season grasses should not receive fertilizer. To sum up briefly, when you use fertilizer-herbicide or fertilizer-insecticide combinations, know which plants you are fertilizing and which you may be killing as well as the right time of year for application.

Aerating and Dethatching the Soil

Grass roots need oxygen as well as moisture, light, and fertilizer in order to grow. This may come as a surprise to many who think of plant roots as being buried and therefore never exposed to the air. But soft, friable soil where roots grow easily and grow long contains a great deal of air. Plant roots take up some oxygen from water, but the main supply of oxygen to plants is the air in the soil. When soil becomes compacted, air circulation is hampered and the result is a haggard, off-color lawn.

Dethatching a lawn

The buildup of thatch on the surface of the soil is a major reason lawns need to be aerated periodically. Thatch is a term used for a layer of undecayed grass that often develops in lawns. Thatch can kill grass and destroy a lawn if it is not removed from time to time.

The lawn grasses generally considered the best are those that produce new plants fairly rapidly while old plants die—a process of constant renewal. As old plants die and decompose, they become the topmost layer of soil. Clippings left on the lawn, especially long clippings from overgrown grass that has been cut back severely, cannot break down in the soil fast enough to avoid hampering the light, moisture, and oxygen requirements of the grass. A prolonged drought will

WEED CONTROL SCHEDULE FOR LAWNS

Weeds	*Time of Application*	*Herbicide*	*Remarks*
Crabgrass, dallisgrass, goosegrass, nutsedge, etc.	May and as needed through summer	DSMA or MSMA (Many different trade names)	Apply 3 to 4 days after mowing, when weeds are 2 to 3 inches tall. Repeat treatment after 7 to 10 days. Do not use on centipedegrass or St. Augustine grass.
Spurge, knotweed mallow, general broadleaf weeds	May and as needed through summer	2, 4-*D* (amine) or 2, 4-*D* + Silvex	Spray to wet the leaves when no rain is expected for 6 to 8 hours. Repeat treatment in 7 to 10 days to control hard-to-kill weeds. Do not apply to St. Augustine grass; may injure centipede.
Annual bluegrass, annual winter weeds	September to November	Dacthal or Azak or Balan or bensulide (Betasan)	Apply before annual bluegrass germinates in the fall. Available as granular formulations. Apply label rate.
Wild garlic, wild onion	November to December	2, 4-*D* (ester or amine)	Apply in late fall before new bulbs are formed. Use detergent or commercial sticker to aid wetting of weed leaves. Also controls emerged annual weeds.
Annual winter weeds: annual bluegrass, chickweed, henbit, clovers, etc.	January or February in the South; March to April in the North	Endothal	Repeat treatment after 7 to 10 days. DO NOT apply to centipedegrass or St. Augustine grass. Apply to other lawn grasses only when DORMANT.
Wild onion, wild garlic	February or March in the South, April to May in the North	2, 4-*D* or 2, 4-*D* + Silvex or dicamba (ester or amine)	Apply second treatment in spring to kill plants which emerged since first application. Continue this program for 3 years to get good results. This schedule will kill other winter weeds except annual bluegrass.
Crabgrass, other annual summer grasses and weeds	March to April	Dacthal or Azak or Balan or bensulide (Betasan)	Apply before weeds and grasses germinate in early spring.

An aerifying machine removes plugs of soil, allowing air and water to penetrate the turf.

also retard the normal breakdown of organic matter. Rapid, excessive growth caused by overfertilizing may also produce a heavy thatch since plant material is being produced more rapidly than it can decompose.

As thatch builds up, the roots of the grass grow in the layer of thatch rather than in the soil. Since thatch dries out rapidly in the hottest months of the summer, the grass dies from lack of moisture. In addition to hindering the supply of air and moisture to plant roots, thatch may harbor insects, pests, and disease-causing fungi.

Thatch buildup varies among lawns. Some lawns seldom if ever develop a thatch layer while others become thatch bound within a few years after the lawn is established.

Thatch development in bluegrass lawns may go undetected for the first 2 or 3 years. The lawn may appear healthy in the spring, then suddenly die in large patches during the hot, dry summer months.

Zoysia, St. Augustine, and Bermuda lawns, though they develop a thatch layer rapidly, seldom die suddenly because they are more resistant than most grasses to the stresses of heat and drought. This is not to say that they do not suffer from thatch; the turf becomes thin and significantly more susceptible to disease.

Thatch can be prevented by good lawn care. Fertilize the soil moderately when you do fertilize; this prevents excessive growth. Mow the lawn regularly and often (weekly) so that severe cutting never becomes necessary. After vacations and other prolonged absences, mow the grass higher than usual, returning it to its normal height through 3 or 4 successive mowings. Rake and remove clippings after you mow. Mowing machines that collect the clippings in a bag for easy disposal are available. The clippings can be composted and turned into a valuable soil conditioner. Water the lawn deeply (for 2 to 4 hours) every 5 to 10 days if there is no rain.

The greatest single deterrrent to thatch buildup is to rake the lawn thoroughly and vigorously before the first flush of new growth begins in early spring. At this time dead grasses are easier to remove than after the new growth emerges. Topdress the lawn every year or two with ¼ inch of compost or weed-free manure to promote the complete decomposition of thatch. Topdressing is effective on most lawn grasses except zoysia.

Removing thatch

To check the lawn for thatch buildup, cut several plugs of soil 2 or 3 inches deep with a pocket knife and remove them. Thatch will appear as a distinct layer of stringy, feltlike material. Zoysia and hybrid Bermudagrasses should be dethatched every year. Bluegrass should be dethatched every other year or when about ⅓ inch of thatch has developed.

Moderate layers of thatch can be removed by vigorous raking with a stiff-toothed garden rake. Thick layers are most efficiently removed by a dethatching or *verticut* machine which you can rent at a garden supply center or a general rental agency. Where thatch buildup has severely damaged large portions of the lawn, mechanical removal of the thatch will also entail removal of much of the living grass. In such extreme cases, it may be wiser to undertake mechanical dethatching in a series of moderate steps extended over a year or two rather than trying to remove it all at once.

Fall Cleanup

Removing fallen leaves promptly is an important step in good lawn maintenance. Grass covered with leaves is deprived of sun and air. Moisture is retained by the leaves, depriving the grass of water. Or, if rainfall is high, the leaves can

Zoysia, Bermuda, and Kentucky bluegrass are particularly prone to problems resulting from thatch buildup. Dethatching machines are available from rental agencies.

The vertical cutting blades of this dethatching machine slice through the layer of uncollected grass clippings and old roots that build up on all lawns. Dethatch the lawn annually.

keep the grass too wet. In addition, the wet leaves encourage the spread of disease organisms.

In the South where the dropping of leaves continues well into winter, raking leaves must become a weekly routine if the leaves are covering the lawn.

There are two ways to look at the task of fall cleanup: performing a chore or harvesting one's compost. The fall's lawn refuse will become spring's new humus for garden soil. Perennial and shrub borders, annual beds, and vegetable gardens all benefit from the addition of compost. So will the lawn. Dry the compost thoroughly and distribute it with spreader. Scratch it into the surface with a lawn rake and water the entire lawn.

How to start a compost pile

To make a compost pile with leaves and fall refuse, you will need to construct a bin. The best materials are wood or cement blocks. Wood should be treated with a nontoxic preservative such as copper napthenate. If you use cement blocks, leave holes in each wall to promote good air circulation in the compost itself.

Spread a layer of leaves, 6 to 12 inches deep, in the bin. Wet the leaves thoroughly. Cover the leaves with enough soil (2 to 4 inches) to weight them down. Sprinkle the layer of leaves and soil with any fertilizer that is high in nitrogen. You can also buy pelleted bacteria which, added to a moist compost pile, help to speed decomposition of the material. Make another layer of leaves, soil, and fertilizer on top of the first, and continue to layer the material, watering the pile as you build. Wet it thoroughly, but not to the point where the soil is washed away.

Active compost heats up, the center of the pile reaching 140° or more within a few days. Keep the pile moist and turn it every 7 to 10 days. Fork the entire pile over, shaking apart matted clumps, and place the less decomposed matter in the center of the pile. You may need to add a little more nitrogen fertilizer if the pile has not decomposed much by the second time you turn it.

Continue to fork the pile over. When the compost no longer heats up after being turned, it is ready to be dried and put on the garden. You may have to turn the pile every day for a few days to dry out. Cover the pile with black polyethylene plastic if rainfall is so heavy that excess moisture prevents the pile from either heating properly at the outset or drying out quickly when decomposition of the material is complete.

Quick compost

Decomposition is much faster if the leaves are first shredded in a leaf shredder or are run over repeatedly with a rotary lawn mower. Alternate layers of shredded leaves or grass clippings with a cup of cottonseed meal, alfalfa meal, or manure to make compost that is ready to use in 1 month. Keep the pile moist and turn it every 4 or 5 days until it no longer heats up.

Not only does compost add new humus to the lawn and garden, it is also a mild fertilizer with a nitrogen, phosphorous, and potassium content comparable to that of cattle or horse manure.

Quick Compost

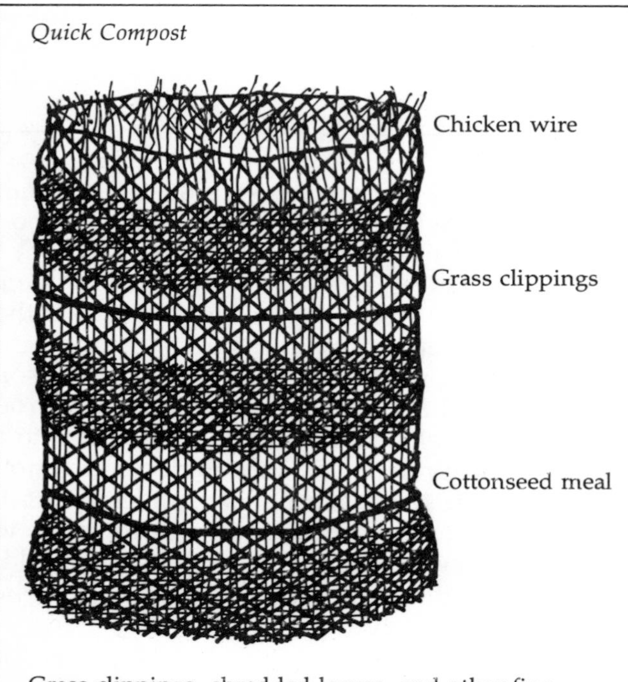

Grass clippings, shredded leaves, and other fine materials can be composted in 2 to 4 weeks. Alternate layers of grass clippings or shredded leaves, covering each 6-inch layer of organic lawn waste with cottonseed meal.

Overseeding Bermuda Lawns for Winter Color

Lawns of common Bermudagrass can be overseeded in the fall with a temporary cool-season grass to keep the lawn green all winter. Common ryegrass is the most popular temporary grass for winter lawns. Inexpensive and readily available, ryegrass establishes rapidly and provides color quickly.

Mow and rake the lawn to be overseeded. Topdress with 5 to 10 pounds of complete fertilizer per 1,000 square feet. Then broadcast ryegrass seed over the area at the rate of 3 to 5 pounds per 1,000 square feet.

With the back of your rake, work the seed through the Bermuda turf into contact with the soil. If possible, topdress with about ⅛-inch of sandy soil or compost, raking it into the turf. Water thoroughly. Keep the soil moist until the grass is established. Keep the wintergrass mowed to a height of 1 to 2 inches. Topdress with 1 to 2 pounds of urea or ammonium nitrate per 1,000 square feet as often as needed to maintain the desired growth and color.

Ryegrass may be competitive with the permanent Bermudagrass on which it is overseeded. This is especially true when the permanent grass is trying to resume growth. For this reason, lower the cutting height in the spring and delay the spring application of nitrogen fertilizer until the ryegrass dies out.

Maintenance of Tools and Equipment

Almost any object made from iron or steel is subject to rusting, but a few simple maintenance measures can prevent costly damage.

Tools and garden equipment that are kept in unheated storage areas are particularly susceptible to rust. Moisture condenses on the cold metal, and if the surface is unprotected, the tool is soon covered with rust. Its surface protection (oil, silicone, wax, or paint) must be checked and replaced continually as it wears away through use.

Perspiration, because it may be slightly acidic, can be another cause of rusting on tool and equipment surfaces. So for maximum protection, wipe down the tool's surfaces with a thin film of oil.

Tools that have become heavily covered with rust should be cleaned by soaking in a liquid rust solvent to loosen the deposits. Use a wire brush to remove all traces of rust without damaging the underlying metal.

To get the best results and longest life from your tools, keep them clean and oiled.

Tools with several parts should be disassembled and cleaned thoroughly. After the rust has been removed, dry all the parts and oil them lightly with a household oil. Silicone spray lubricants are also available and convenient to use.

During the winter, have the blades of your lawn mower sharpened. Dull blades not only decrease the efficiency of the mower, making mowing even more of a chore, they can also damage grass plants by making ragged cuts on the leaves. This often results in browning or shredding of the grass leaves.

Clean all power equipment thoroughly. Use a wire brush to remove caked on dirt, grass clippings, and other refuse. Your attention to maintenance will spare you the aggravation of inefficient equipment and the expense of replacing it.

Recognizing and Treating Lawn Problems

Common Lawn Problems

Lawn grasses, like other plants, have their problems. However, few types of plants have received as much attention from plant breeders as lawn grasses. Lawn grasses have been bred to be walked on. This fact alone indicates that lawn grasses are tougher than most herbaceous plants and can withstand many abuses. Nonetheless, lawn grasses are not indestructible. Much depends on the person who tends the lawn. Most important of all is proper preparation of the soil when the lawn is built.

Because we spend a lot of time on our lawns, we often notice problems sooner than we would with other types of plantings. Immediate corrective action is the key to overcoming growth problems. Eliminating a small infestation of chinch bugs is obviously easier than eliminating a large population of this destructive insect. Equally important, the smaller the area damaged, the quicker the recovery. Left to their own devices, chinch bugs can ravage vast areas of the lawn. It may take all summer for the lawn to regain its pleasing appearance.

Some common lawn ailments, their symptoms, and recommended control measures are described in this chapter. No homeowner is likely to be beset with every problem discussed, but we include most common problems here for reference. Whenever problems arise, do not hesitate to call on your county agricultural extension agent for advice. His number is in the telephone directory under the listings for your county government.

Scalping occurs when grass on a mound or ridge is cut shorter than the surrounding grass. Cut nearly to the ground, these areas may turn yellow or brown, lose vigor, and attract insects and fungus diseases. In early spring before active growth begins you can better see poorly graded spots; level all humps and ridges and fill in depressions.

Fertilizing problems are not uncommon. Pale color and poor vigor usually indicate a need for fertilizer. Streaking and burned-looking areas indicate overfertilization. Adjust your fertilizer schedule and rates to promote the best growth. If fertilizer burn occurs, water damaged spots thoroughly to wash excess fertilizer down into the soil. Always apply chemical fertilizers with caution.

Frayed grass blades accompanied by a general browning of the lawn is due to dull mower blades. Grass plants damaged in this way never fully recover between mowings and are more prone to insect and disease attack. Have your mower blades sharpened at least once a year.

Bare soil due to drainage or erosion should be turned to loosen it, then leveled with additional topsoil and reseeded. Apply a light mulch of hay, pine straw, or peat moss to keep the seed and soil in place. If possible, divert the flow of water into a drainage ditch, or else into a more dispersed pattern of flow.

Mosses and algae rarely develop on a healthy lawn. The most common causes of their presence in lawns are inadequate fertilization and poor drainage. Other causes include high soil acidity, improper watering, too much shade, soil compaction, or a combination of all of these. A soil test should be made to determine the precise cause. Remove moss and algae by raking them or by burning them off with ferrous sulfate. Apply the ferrous sulfate to the moss spots in concentrated amounts when the moss is damp. Do not wash it into the soil. Lime sprinkled on the surface will control moss until turf can grow back. Both moss and algae will return, however, if the cause is not corrected.

Dog urine damage can be irritating, especially when the cause is someone else's dog. Affected spots in the lawn are usually round or slightly irregular with the grass turning from straw-colored to brown. This injury may be mistaken for damage from brown patch disease. In severe cases that are left untreated the grass may die. Water heavily to leach urine residues out of the surface soil.

Late spring frosts can damage tender young growth on lawn grass plants. Because food for the entire plant is stored in all parts of the plant, the killing of new growth destroys much of the plant's food reserve. Several frosts, separated by warm periods that permit new growth, may completely exhaust the food reserves and kill the plant. In less severe cases, roots of damaged plants fail to develop adequately and the turf becomes thin and unthrifty. Most grasses will recover from one or two unseasonal frosts. Frost-damaged centipedegrass responds well to a light feeding of iron chelate or ferrous sulfate.

Wilting is usually caused by inadequate water. If wilting is accompanied by inward rolling of leaf blades, dullness of color, and loss of resiliency, water the lawn thoroughly. The lawn has lost resiliency if you can see your footprints after walking across it. During periods of sparse rainfall, water the lawn every 7 to 10 rainless days. Lawns on sandy soil may need watering every 4 or 5 days during hot, dry weather.

Yellowing can be caused by a number of factors: iron deficiency, underfertilization, overfertilization, too much lime. The most likely cause of yellowing is iron deficiency or chlorosis. Several turf grasses display symptoms of chlorosis, but it is most common on centipedegrass. Overfertilization produces fast, luxuriant growth, but can also rob plants of available iron in the soil. Grass that enters the winter in a weakened, chlorotic condition is liable to be slow in reestablishing an adequate root system in the spring. Chlorotic symptoms (yellow blades with green veins) may appear early in the growing season and then disappear when the condition is not too severe. Adding lime without the recommendation of a soil test can result in an overabundance of lime in the soil, another condition that can rob plants of iron. Late fall drought also has a chlorotic effect. Damage from late fall drought often goes unnoticed because homeowners think that the yellowing and browning of the grass are simply indications of approaching winter dormancy. But the grass is severely weakened when it actually does become dormant.

Chlorosis can be cured by adding iron chelate or ferrous sulfate. Applied as a soil drench or foliar spray, either relieves the symptoms of chlorotic yellowing in 3 to 5 days.

Compacted soil is common in the Southeast and in other sections of the country where soil has a high clay content. When soil becomes so packed down that water can't penetrate, the grass will thin out and bare spots may result. Soil compaction can be prevented or corrected by aerating (punching holes in the surface of the soil) at least once a year. Aerifying machines and other equipment are available from garden supply centers and general rental agencies.

Seed rot in new lawns may be the result of excessively moist soil, especially in hot humid weather when the fungi *Pythium* and *Rhizoctonia* are most active. These fungi attack newly sown seed and cause young seedlings that do germinate to grow poorly. The grass stand may be thin and sickly, growing in irregular patches. Affected areas are often invaded by weeds. To prevent seed rot, buy top quality seed and treat it, before planting, with a general fungicide such as thiram or Captan. Use ½ teaspoon of fungicide per pound of seed. Eliminate depressions in the soil and other areas where drainage may be poor. Avoid seeding during hot, moist weather; early fall and early spring are the best times to seed.

Buried debris, especially around new construction sites, can hamper plant growth. A thin layer of soil over rocks, chunks of plaster, boards, or cement dries out rapidly and may not contain enough moisture to keep grass green. Dig around in areas where growth is poor to see if buried debris is the problem. If it is, dig up all troublesome debris, rework the soil, and replant.

Mottled green and brown lawn may be the result of a poor mixture of grass varieties. Warm-season grasses turn brown after the first killing frost while cool-season grasses remain green. The effect often resembles a diseased lawn. To ascertain whether your problem is simply a bad seed mixture, compare blades of the green grass with blades of the browned grass. If they are not markedly different in character, the problem may be brown patch disease.

Centipede decline is commonly characterized by the failure of centipede lawns to green up in the spring. Factors thought to contribute to this problem include high soil phosphorus levels, high or very low soil pH, high nitrogen applications, heavy thatch, compacted sod, winterkill, insect damage, and mowing too high.

These factors may act independently or interact to cause the problem.

First, try to determine the cause of the problem and then take action. Remove thatch in the dead areas, and roto-till the soil to a depth of about 6 inches. Resprig or seed at the recommended rate and keep watered to help establish the grass.

Withhold any fertilizer or lime applications from the newly established grass unless a soil test indicates otherwise. Maintain a mowing height of 1 to 1½ inches and remove all clippings from the lawn.

Unidentifiable problems can worry the homeowner most of all. Inspect the lawn carefully for infestations of insects or diseases; then call the county agricultural extension agent (whose number is listed under your county government) and describe your lawn problems. Chances are the agent will suggest a soil test in addition to control measures for your lawn problem. Take this advice; a soil test virtually eliminates the guesswork from dealing with lawn problems. Ask for details on where to send your soil sample to be tested. In addition to the soil testing laboratory of your state department of agriculture, you will find many garden supply stores that also test soil.

Fungus Diseases

There are no simple formulae for growing a healthy lawn. Attentive care, including mowing, watering, fertilizing, and insect control, is the surest way to have a lawn you can be proud of. But all plants, lawn grasses included, are susceptible to various diseases. A basic understanding of the causes of some of these diseases will help you overcome them and restore your lawn to good health.

First, most diseases are caused by fungi that reproduce by means of spores. These spores are spread by wind, water, infected grass clippings, mowers, and a number of other ways. To grow and spread infection, most fungi require moist conditions. For this reason, lawn diseases are most common and most harmful during wet, humid seasons.

Other factors that can influence the occurrence and spread of diseases on your lawn include time of watering, removal of grass clippings, height of mowing, air circulation, and susceptibility of grass varieties.

Watering late in the day is bad for lawn grasses because the plants will remain wet all night, thereby encouraging the growth of mildew and other fungi.

Grass clippings left on the lawn after mowing also retain moisture on the surface of the lawn. If fungi do not develop, the clippings can become matted and form a dense layer (called thatch) on the surface of the soil, hampering moisture penetration and further encouraging the growth of fungi.

Mowing height is also important. Mow frequently enough so that you never need to remove more than ⅓ of the top growth at one time. Mow upright grasses to about 2 inches, creeping grasses, such as bentgrass or the Bermudas, to a height of ½ to 1 inch.

Mixtures of grass seed are more effective in thwarting diseases than pure stands of a single variety. The reason for this is that a disease can damage only the susceptible varieties in a stand of grass. The entire stand is never decimated. The resistant varieties continue to grow and thrive, keeping the lawn green while damaged varieties recover. If you intend to plant a pure stand of grass, check with the county agricultural extension agent to find out which varieties are the most resistant to fungus diseases that may be prevalent in your area.

When using fungicides, use them with caution. As with other garden chemicals, store fungicides well out of the reach of children and pets. Do not feed clippings of fungicide treated grass to livestock.

Here are some common fungus diseases, their symptoms, and their controls.

Brown patch

This fungus disease is particularly destructive in moist, cool weather but can also occur in warm weather. Circular brown patches of various sizes appear in diseased grass. Although the grass will usually recover, under extreme conditions the disease can kill or weaken runners to such an extent that they are susceptible to other harmful organisms. The symptoms are sometimes mistaken for chinch bug damage, but chinch bugs completely kill areas of infestation. In areas attacked by brown patch, green spots will remain.

A management practice recommended for controlling brown patch is to avoid buildup of thatch. The causal fungus may become established in this accumulation of grass clippings and, under favorable conditions, attack healthy grass.

Brown patch may be controlled by spraying the affected area and immediately adjacent areas thoroughly with a fungicide containing PCNB (pentachloronitrobenzene) or Tersan. Apply according to the manufacturer's directions.

Cottony blight, grease spot

These diseases, caused by the fungus *Pythium*, occur on many lawn grasses and are most likely to occur in the humid areas of the country. Cottony blight is especially common on temporary ryegrass lawns in the South. The fungi are destructive at 70°F. and above, especially in poorly drained soil. New turf is particularly susceptible to *Pythium* diseases but under the right conditions any lawn can be affected.

Pythium injury is most apparent in early morning as a circular spot or group of spots about 2 inches in diameter surrounded by blackened grass blades that are intertwined with the fungus threads. Diseased leaves mat together and become slimy. The darkened grass blades wither and become reddish brown, particularly in sunny or windy weather. Affected grass dies within 24 hours and lies flat on the ground rather than remaining upright as does grass damaged by brown patch disease. New grass does not grow back into the diseased area. The diseased areas may vary from a few inches to several feet in diameter, often appearing as streaks as though the fungus was spread by mowing or by water flow following heavy rains.

Preventive measures against *Pythium* diseases start with assuring good drainage in the lawn area. Avoid watering methods that keep either the grass or the ground wet for long periods. Avoid excessive watering, especially during hot, humid weather. Delay seeding until fall whenever possible as cool, dry weather generally checks the disease.

Fungicides recommended for control of *Pythium* diseases include zineb and Dexon. Repeat applications every 5 to 14 days until control is complete.

Dollar spot

Also known as *small brown patch*, dollar spot is caused by the fungus *Sclerotinia*. This fungus may attack many species of lawn grasses but is most destructive in bentgrasses, especially in the humid regions of the North and East. Attack is most likely during the cool, wet weather of May and June and September and October. Though even well-kept, fertile lawns may be plagued by dollar spot, nitrogen-deficient lawns seem the hardest hit.

The usual symptom of *Sclerotinia* damage is a series of bleached spots the size of a silver dollar. Sometimes the diseased areas merge to form irregular patches. Affected grass is killed and the turf left pitted. In early stages of infection, the diseased spots are dark and wet in appearance, turning light brown and nearly white as the fungus develops. During the periods of active growth, the fungus can be detected in the early morning while the dew is still on the grass as a fine, white cobweblike mycelium. Sometimes only the uppermost grass leaves are affected, developing light-colored blotches.

Turf can recover quickly from dollar spot if it is treated in the early stages of attack. Otherwise it may take several weeks for new grass to become established in the dead areas.

Fungicides recommended for control of dollar spot include Acti-dione-thiram, Daconil 2787, and Fore.

Leaf spot, foot rots

Caused by the *Helminthosporium* fungus, leaf spot is one of the most destructive and widespread of grass diseases. Kentucky bluegrasses are those most frequently attacked. Development of the fungus is most obvious during cool, moist spring and fall weather, but attack may also occur in the summer.

Although damage is most apparent on the leaves, the entire plant is attacked. Leaves have reddish brown to purplish black spots. Stems, crowns, rhizomes, and roots discolor and rot. Injury is often mistaken for drought damage and goes untreated. Crabgrass and other weeds invade the damaged areas as lawn grasses die out.

As with many fungus diseases, leaf spot and foot rot are best prevented by good cultural practices: mowing, watering, and fertilizing. Also, some varieties are more resistant than others. Common Kentucky bluegrass is particularly susceptible to leaf spot and foot rots. Resistant varieties include 'Merion', 'Fylking', 'Pennstar', and 'Windsor', though even these are not 100 percent resistant.

Fungicides recommended for controlling leaf spot and foot rots include Act-dione-thiram, Captan, Fore, Daconil 2787, and zineb.

Rust

Rust fungi attack Kentucky bluegrass and zoysia lawns from Rhode Island to California and from southern Canada to Oklahoma. Symptoms usually appear in late summer and remain until frost. Heavy dew favors development.

Symptoms to watch for include yellow orange or red brown powdery pustules on leaves and stems of grass. Rub a cloth over affected leaves; the rust colored spores will produce a yellow or orange stain.

Good watering, mowing, and fertilizing practices are the best preventive measures against rust. No chemical completely eradicates rust, but control can be effected with Acti-dione-thiram or zineb. Both tend to injure 'Merion' bluegrass temporarily and to retard growth for a week or so. Injury is temporary, however, with normal growth resuming in 1 to 2 weeks. Repeated applications may be necessary on 'Merion' bluegrass to keep rust under control.

Pure stands of 'Merion' bluegrass, 'Emerald' zoysia, and 'Meyer' zoysia are most susceptible to rust. Common Kentucky bluegrass is fairly resistant to rust but is vulnerable to the more destructive *Helminthosporium* leaf spot fungus. Mixing 'Merion' bluegrass equally with common bluegrass or with red fescue produces a turf that resists rust well.

Stripe smut

Stripe smut is a serious fungus disease of bluegrasses, particularly in the northern half of the United States. Smut is especially devastating on young seedling grasses of new lawns. This disease, caused by the fungus *Ustilago*, is most noticeable during cool weather in spring and fall. Diseased Kentucky bluegrass plants may occur singly or in spots from a few inches to a foot or more in diameter. Plants are often pale green to yellow and are shorter than neighboring healthy plants. Narrow gray or black stripes develop lengthwise on leaf blades. The gray stripes are unruptured masses of spores called *sori*. Black stripes occur as the sori rupture and spill spores along the leaf blades. Following rupture of the sori, diseased leaves wither, curl, and shred from the tips downward. The plants then die.

'Merion' is the variety most susceptible to stripe smut. Incidence of smut in bluegrass lawns can be reduced by planting a mixture of 'Merion' with common bluegrass or with smut-tolerant varieties such as 'Fylking', 'Park', or 'Pennstar'. The only fungicide currently recommended for the control of stripe smut is Tersan 1991.

Mushrooms

Mushrooms in themselves are not harmful to the lawn, but they may indicate the presence of fairy ring, a minor fungus disease. If the mushrooms are merely the result of prolonged wet weather and have grown upon buried pieces of wood or other organic matter, dig them up along with the debris to which they are attached. Where this is not possible, drench the soil around the mushrooms with a solution of Captan. Use an iron rod to punch holes 6 to 8 inches deep in the area around the mushrooms, then pour in the Captan solution.

Fairy ring

Fairy rings are circles or arcs of dark green grass surrounding areas of light colored or dead grass. During spring and fall mushrooms develop along the outline of the fairy ring. Unless the fungus (several genera of *Basidiomycetes*) is controlled, the ring enlarges each year, leaving alternate bands of green and discolored grass. Depending on moisture and soil conditions, the band may spread from 6 to 24 inches each year. Fairy rings are not permanently destructive; the problem usually cures itself if good cultural practices are followed.

Fading out of St. Augustine grass

A condition called fading out is frequently a serious problem with St. Augustine grass during the summer months. A fungus disease is involved, but it is believed that the fungus is active only on grass that is weakened by other causes.

Conditions that contribute to the problem of fading out are excessively wet weather, shade both from cloud cover and from trees, soil compaction caused by water either standing or draining over the surface of the ground, and root competition for food from the trees and shrubs in the area. Correcting these conditions and spraying the lawn with an all-purpose fungicide, such as zineb or Captan, will help to eliminate fading out.

Slime mold

Though slime molds are not destructive fungi, they are unsightly on grass. The blades become covered with tiny cottonlike swabs of blue, black, or yellow. Slime molds appear during wet weather, then disappear as soon as dry conditions prevail. Sweep over the grass with a broom or else spray the grass with a strong stream of water from the garden hose to break up the masses of fungus material that cling to the grass.

Powdery mildew

A lawn badly infected with mildew looks as if it has been dusted with flour. Infected leaves usually turn yellow and wither. The occurrence of powdery mildew is most common in the fall and spring when nights are cool. Mildew is most severe in shaded, damp areas. Uncontrolled, powdery mildew can severely damage, even kill, extensive areas of the lawn.

Mildew is caused by the fungus *Erysiphe*. Attaching itself to the leaves, the fungus sends suckerlike structures into the leaf cells to obtain nourishment. The aerial portion of the fungus produces thousands of spores which are distributed by water and wind.

Healthy, vigorous lawns on well-drained soil are seldom bothered by powdery mildew. Control of the disease begins by restoring good maintenance practices. Fungicides recommended for control include Acti-dione-thiram, Benlate, and Karathane. Make 2 applications about 10 days apart. If possible, reduce shade in affected areas by pruning dense trees and shrubs.

Snow mold, fusarium patch

These diseases, caused by the fungi *Typhula* and *Fusarium*, are most destructive on bentgrasses, though they may also attack other lawn grasses. Snow mold, also called winter scald, is most severe when green, actively growing grass is suddenly covered by snow. Fusarium patch may occur during the growing season when humidity is high but daytime temperatures are cool. Any condition that keeps the turf excessively wet encourages the spread of these diseases.

Snow mold first appears as a white, cottony growth on the leaves. As leaves die they turn light brown and cling together. Diseased areas are usually 1 to 12 inches or more in diameter and dirty white, gray, or slightly pink in color.

Fusarium patch is characterized by irregular pale yellow areas from several inches to several feet in diameter. Affected areas later become whitish gray, often with a faint pink edge.

Fall care will determine the susceptible condi-

GUIDE FOR SELECTING FUNGICIDES

Disease and Causal Organism	*Fungicide*	*Directions*
Leaf spot (Blight, Going-out, Melting-out) *Helminthosporium*	Acti-dione-thiram Captan Daconil 2787 Dyrene Fore Zineb	Disease can appear from April to August, depending on kind of grass and species of fungus. Treat your lawn every 7 to 14 days three times consecutively or until the disease has been controlled.
Brown Patch *Rhizoctonia solani*	Dyrene Fore PCNB	Disease can appear from June to August. Treat your lawn every 5 to 10 days until the disease has been controlled.
Rust *Puccinia*	Acti-dione-thiram Daconil 2787 Zineb	Disease can appear from June to September. Treat your lawn every 7 to 14 days until rust disappears.
Grease Spot and Cottony Blight *Pythium*	Dexon Zineb	Disease can appear from July to September and in fall and winter during warm, humid periods in the South. Treat your lawn every 5 to 14 days until the disease has been controlled.
Dollar Spot *Sclerotinia*	Acti-dione-thiram Daconil 2787 Dyrene Fore	Disease can appear from June to October. Treat your lawn at 7 to 14 day intervals until the disease has been controlled.
Stripe Smut *Ustilago*	Tersan 1991	Apply in October or early spring before grass begins growing.
Snow Mold *Typhula*	Dyrene	Water lawn well after applying.
Fusarium Patch *Fusarium*	Tersan 1991	Disease can appear from fall to spring. Treat your lawn at intervals of 2 to 6 weeks as needed.
Slime Molds *Physarum cinereum*	Fore Zineb	Disease can appear throughout the growing season and can be controlled without fungicides.

United States Department of Agriculture

CAUTION: Do not feed clippings to livestock or poultry.

Fungicide recommendations are subject to change. For the most up-to-date recommendations, consult your county agricultural extension agent.

tion of the turf as it goes into winter. Withhold late fall fertilizer that might stimulate tender new leaves that are actively growing when snow covers the ground. Keep the lawn cut in the fall to prevent grass from matting. Apply lime if a soil test indicates high soil acidity.

No fungicide completely controls snow mold or fusarium patch. Dyrene, however, can reduce the severity of the damage. Apply Dyrene before the first lasting snow. Additional treatments may be necessary if snow melts in midwinter or in early spring.

Gray leaf spot

This disease, caused by the fungus *Piricularia*, is most severe in hot, humid areas. St. Augustine grasses are most severely affected, developing irregular brown or gray spots on leaf blades. Shaded areas that tend to remain damp are the most likely to develop gray leaf spot. In severely damaged areas the grass may appear burned or scorched due to the mass spotting of leaf blades.

Newly sprigged grass is particularly susceptible to gray leaf mold, as are lawns that are growing too rapidly due to overfertilization. Withhold nitrogen fertilizer if you suspect gray leaf spot in your lawn. Avoid watering late in the day; water early enough so that the turf can dry out before nightfall.

Gray leaf spot can be effectively controlled with zineb, Thiram, Acti-dione-thiram, or Dyrene.

Common Insect Pests

Lawn grasses, like other garden plants, are very attractive to insects. Some insects feed on the roots of grass, others feed on leaves or stems. Still others suck juices from the leaves, thereby crippling the plants. As a result of damage by these pests, the grass generally becomes discolored and takes on a ragged appearance. Heavy infestations can result in the death of the entire lawn.

The extent of damage caused by insects depends on such factors as temperature, humidity, rainfall, soil conditions, susceptibility of the grass, soil fertility, and cultural practices such as proper mowing and dethatching.

For the new homeowner insect control may seem to entail a lot of guesswork, but once he learns to recognize problems in their earliest stage, his ability to control insect infestations will become increasingly efficient. Don't hesitate to consult the county agricultural extension agent (look in the telephone directory under your county government) to find out what problems are prevalent in your area or what to do about problems you already have. Whenever you find insects you cannot identify, collect them in a small glass jar to show the retailer at the garden supply center. This, better than a description, will enable him to identify the insect and recommend control measures.

Control by prevention

Healthy lawns are generally less subject to attack by insects than are ragged, poorly fertilized and poorly drained lawns. The following are some tips on good cultural practices that will minimize insect problems and assure early detection of problems that do arise:

- Do not overfertilize, especially during hot, humid weather.
- To prevent a buildup of thatch, collect all clippings after mowing an established lawn.
- Apply water only when grass wilts slightly or shows other signs of a need for moisture. When you do water, water deeply.
- Collect soil samples in the fall and have them tested by the state soil testing laboratory. This takes the guesswork out of liming and fertilizing.
- Mow the lawn weekly. The recommended height for upright grasses is 1½ to 2 inches, for creeping grasses, ½ to 1 inch.

When insect infestations do appear, you may need to use an insecticide to control them. Early detection and early control measures will enable you to effect the most complete control and, it is hoped, to confine the infestation to as limited an area as possible.

How to use insecticides

First, measure the length and width of the lawn; then multiply the length by the width to determine the area of the lawn in square feet.

Select the appropriate insecticide (see chart at end of chapter) and figure out how much insecticide to apply to the infested area. Insecticides are commercially available as granules, dusts, or emulsifiable concentrates.

Granules may be applied by hand, with a cyclone seeder, or with a fertilizer spreader. If you apply the granules by hand, use a quart jar with holes punched in the lid.

Dusts may be applied with a hand duster, or you can simply sprinkle the dust by hand over the infested area. After applying the dust, brush the grass leaves with the back of a rake to distribute the dust more evenly and to filter it through the leaves to stems and crowns of plants. Then water the entire lawn area to wash the fertilizer into the root zone of the soil. Do not apply dusts when the grass is wet.

Emulsifiable concentrates are dissolved in water and applied as sprays. Label directions will tell you exactly how much insecticide to use for a specific area. For small areas, use an old plastic jug that can be discarded after use. If you use a watering can to apply insecticide solutions, wash the can out thoroughly after use. Hand sprayers are also sufficient for applying insecticides in limited areas. For large areas, it may be best to use a compressed air sprayer which you can rent from garden supply centers or general rental agencies.

The way you apply insecticides depends on the type of insects you hope to control. Lawn insects are roughly divided into two groups: *below ground* and *above ground* insects. (See chart at end of chapter.) To control below ground insects, the insecticide must penetrate the soil. To control above ground insects, apply insecticides so as to get thorough coverage of grass blades, stems, and ground surface with as little wash-off and soil penetration as possible. Hose sprayers are excellent for applying insecticides and fungicides on lawns.

Insecticide Sprayers

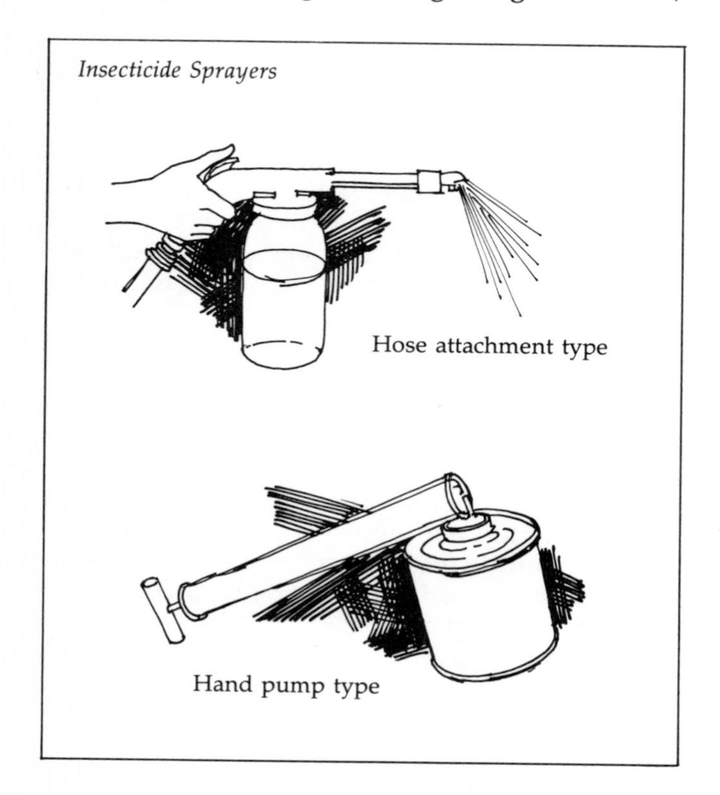

Other Pests

Moles, pocket gophers, field mice, and other small animals may cause damage to the lawn by burrowing under the turf. These pests are usually looking for insects and grubs, so a lawn that is maintained on a good insect control program is less likely to be plagued by small rodents. Holes in the lawn indicate the presence of small burrowing rodents.

Traps in mole tunnels are the best method of controlling moles. Poison baits will control pocket gophers and field mice but are not effective on moles. Traps and baits are available at most hardware stores or lawn and garden supply centers.

Nematodes are microscopic creatures that live primarily in the soil. Many are beneficial, but some are plant parasites that inhabit the root systems of plants, including lawn grasses.

Nematodes are often the cause of poor quality lawns. In some areas Bermudagrass, zoysiagrass, and centipedegrass cannot be grown satisfactorily unless nematodes are controlled.

Since nematodes cannot be seen with the naked eye, diagnosis is difficult. Symptoms to observe include off-color blades of grass, somewhat yellow and stunted. The turf will usually be thin and in an unthrifty state of growth. The grass often appears to be suffering from lack of fertilizer or water but will not respond to applications of either.

Carefully examine the roots of the grass for signs of abnormal growth. Affected roots will appear shriveled, blackened, and stubby. There will generally be an absence of white feeder roots.

All of the common lawn grasses may be affected by nematodes. Bahiagrass appears to be least affected.

There are many different types of nematodes that parasitize lawn grasses. This makes nematode control a difficult problem since one type may be easily killed while another type may not be as easy to destroy.

If nematodes are suspected, contact your local county agricultural extension agent for advice on collecting specimens and information on where to send them for a positive identification and proper methods of control.

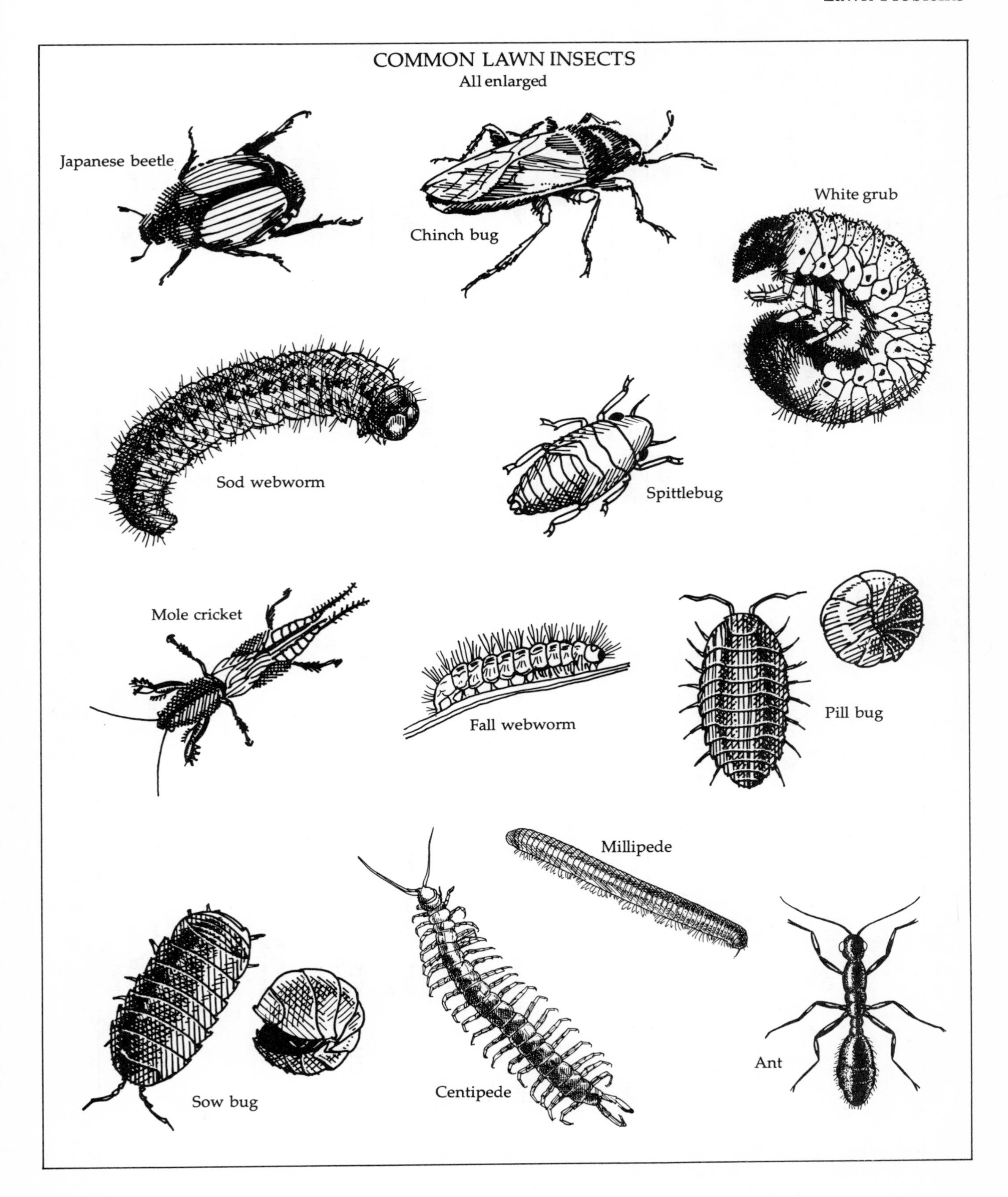
COMMON LAWN INSECTS
All enlarged
Japanese beetle
Chinch bug
White grub
Sod webworm
Spittlebug
Mole cricket
Fall webworm
Pill bug
Millipede
Sow bug
Centipede
Ant

LAWN INSECT CONTROL GUIDE

Insect	*Description*	*Susceptible Grasses*	*Damage*	*Pesticide*
BELOW GROUND PESTS				
White grubs	Plump, C-shaped grubs. Whitish or grayish with darker hind parts and brown heads. Generally found 1 to 3 inches underground in mild weather. Adults known as May or June beetles.	Most lawn grasses	Feed on roots and cut them off below soil surface. Grass turns yellow and then brown, often in irregular patches. Where damage is heavy, mats of turf can be pulled back like a carpet.	chlordane* A single application
Ants	Several species. Build nests in the ground; some form hills around nest openings. Some, such as fire and harvester ants, sting people and animals.	Most lawn grasses	Ant hills and mounds are unsightly and often smother surrounding grass. Ants may damage roots of grass by nesting about them and also destroy grass seeds in the ground preventing good stands.	chlordane* Diazinon
Mole crickets	Light brown; body covered with fine hair; velvety appearance. About 1½ inches long. Front legs short and flattened, adapted for burrowing.	Bermuda, zoysia, St. Augustine	Feed on roots of grass. Burrowing in soil uproots seedlings and causes soil to dry out quickly. Most serious in newly planted areas but also damage established turf.	chlordane*, carbaryl (Sevin), Diazinon, toxaphene
Cicada-killer wasps	About 1½ inches long with yellow and black markings. May sting people if molested.	Most lawn grasses	Dig deep nests or burrows in the ground and mound the soil at nest entrance.	chlordane*
Ground pearls	Immature or nymph stage of soil-inhabiting scale insects. Nymphs encysted in hard, globular shells that resemble tiny pearls about ¼ inch in diameter.	Bermuda, centipede, St. Augustine	Feed on fine grass rootlets by sucking plant juices. When infestations are heavy, grass turns brown and dies in irregular spots.	Dansanit
ABOVE GROUND PESTS				
Chinch bugs	Adults are about ¹⁄₆ inch long. Body flattened, narrow, and black in color. White wings with black triangular patch at middle of outer margin. Young (nymphs) are smaller and reddish with a white band across the back.	Bluegrass, bentgrass, St. Augustine	Suck plant juices from grasses and cause brown spots with yellow margins in lawns.	Aspon, carbaryl (Sevin), Diazinon, ethion
Armyworms	Green caterpillars when small; dark brown and about 1½ inches long when grown; adults are moths. Body has dark stripes along each side and down the center of the back. Inverted *Y* marking on head.	Most lawn grasses	Feed on blades of grass, causing ragged and off-color appearance. When numerous, they may devour grass down to ground, leaving circular bare areas. Damage often in irregular pattern in lawn.	chlordane*, carbaryl (Sevin), Diazinon, toxaphene

LAWN INSECT CONTROL GUIDE

Insect	*Description*	*Susceptible Grasses*	*Damage*	*Pesticide*
Spittlebugs	Adults are wedge shaped, about 1/4 inch long. Dark brown or black with two orange stripes on wings. Nymphs are ivory and live in masses of a bubbly froth or "spittle" in grass.	Most lawn grasses	Suck sap from grasses, cause discoloration, and stunt growth. Adults also feed on foliage of various shrubs.	carbaryl (Sevin), malathion, methoxychlor
Sod webworms	Larvae are dingy white to light brown, marked with dark spots. Mature larvae about 3/4 inch long. Live in silken webs just beneath the soil surface.Silk-lined tunnels of earth near the soil surface are evidence of this pest.	Bluegrass, Bermuda, St. Augustine	Larvae feed on grass foliage, chewing and ragging blades of grass. Damage usually occurs in patches.	Same recommendations as for armyworms above.
Millipedes and centipedes	Wormlike animals with many body segments and usually dark brown. Millipedes have two pairs of legs on each segment; centipedes have one pair per segment. Coil body into small ball when disturbed.	Most lawn grasses	Do not usually damage lawns; feed chiefly on decaying matter. Sometimes congregate in yards after heavy rains. Can become nuisance when numerous by crawling into houses, garages, swimming pools, etc.	Same recommendations as for armyworms above.
Sowbugs and pillbugs	Light gray to slate colored animals. Segmented body about 1/2 inch long with seven pairs of legs. When disturbed, they roll up into tiny balls.	Most lawn grasses	Feed on organic matter in soil and sometimes on grass and other plants. Seldom cause serious injury but are nuisance in damp areas in and around yard; may enter houses.	chlordane*
Chiggers	Chiggers or red bugs are tiny red mites that invade lawns from surrounding grassy or woody areas. So small that they are seldom seen.	Most lawn grasses	Are annoying to people. Attach themselves temporarily to the skin and cause severe irritation and intense itching.	chlordane,* sulfur, Diazinon, malathion, toxaphene
Clover mites	Reddish brown mites smaller than the head of straight pin.	Most cool-season grasses	Feed on clover, grasses, shrubs, and other plants but do not cause serious damage. Occur in tremendous numbers and can be objectionable pests entering homes in spring, summer, and early fall.	malathion, Diazinon

U. S. Department of Agriculture

*Presently under regulatory hearings

Ground Covers and How To Use Them

Ground covers, as the name suggests, are plants that are massed together to cover ground. Lawn grasses are the most commonly used ground covers, but lawn grasses are not practical in all home planting situations. Sharp slopes, shady areas, or areas too large to easily manage as a lawn can be made graceful and attractive with other ground cover plants. In this capacity, ground covers are great problem solvers in the home landscape. In addition, swerving beds of ground cover contrast pleasingly with the lawn and make both more distinctive.

The selection of attractive ground covers is vast. For every soil type, light exposure, or fertility level, there is a ground cover that will thrive. Most important, once you have planted a ground cover, the annual maintenance required will take only a fraction of the time you would spend mowing and grooming a lawn of the same area. This is not to say that ground covers require no attention. All plants require adequate water, fertilizer, and weed control. But the fact is that a well-kept ground cover planting is one of the least demanding home landscape features.

... Solvers

...tion of ground cov-
...ving carpet for bare
...are, it erodes, espe-
...sn't erode becomes
... are nature's own
...are ground can be-
...er weeds nor desir-
... extreme cases this
...ecome a collection
...om the rest of the
...e growth of algae.
...e more than a deco-

...ad by means of un-
...omes), and others
... (stolons) over the
...at spread by above
... for covering rocky
...ufficiently to allow
...n grasses.

...larly useful in solv-
...ich include filling
...atios, covering ex-
... carpet for particu-
...ky or uneven land, covering steep slopes and banks, serving as an underplanting for bulbous plants, especially lilies and iris, and binding sandy soils where erosion may be a particular problem. Look around your yard and garden. You may discover a number of other situations where ground covers can solve home landscaping problems.

Selecting Ground Covers

In selecting ground cover plants, you must take into account the growth habit of the plants as well as the growth conditions you can provide. Plants that spread rapidly may be more difficult to keep in bounds than slow-growing plants. Plants with extensive root systems and underground stems may be difficult to establish in rocky areas or in tight, clay soil. Height of mature plants is also important.

Growth conditions include climate, light conditions, soil type, moisture, and drainage. The Plant Hardiness Zone Map at the front of the book will help you determine whether or not the plants you wish to grow are suited to your climate. Soil conditions can be altered to meet the requirements of the plants. Soil can be made more acid by the addition of organic matter, especially pine needles, shredded pine bark, or peat moss. Excessively acid soil can be made more neutral by adding lime to the soil. Drainage can be improved in clay soils by adding sand and organic matter. Moisture retention in sandy soils can be improved by adding organic matter, especially peat moss.

Ornamental characteristics of ground covers include foliage shape and color, flower color, and season of bloom. Foliage may remain on plants year round (evergreen), or the plants may lose their leaves or die back in the fall (deciduous), then resume growth the following spring.

Some ground cover plants may be evergreen in the mild climates of the South and West, but deciduous in areas where the temperature drops significantly below freezing.

Liriope (*L. muscari*) is a superb low-maintenance ground cover for small areas.

Three ground cover plants and their uses: asiatic jasmine in a small island planting and along the low brick wall, santolina at the corner of the island and cascading over the wall beside the steps, and cinquefoil between the steps and sections of pavement.

Ajuga planted here will conceal the drainage outlet without hampering its functionality.

Ground covers for seashore gardens

Not all plants adapt well to the dry soil and salty, windy air of the seashore. Among those plants that are best suited, the following are popular and dependable:

Beach wormwood	*Artemisia stelleriana*
Bearberry	*Arctostaphylos uva-ursi*
Cinquefoil	*Potentilla tridentata*
Cotoneaster	*Cotoneaster* sp.
Daylily	*Hemerocallis* sp.
Hall's honeysuckle	*Lonicera japonica halliana*
Heath	*Erica carnea*
Heather	*Calluna vulgaris*
Juniper	*Juniperus* sp.
Lantana	*Lantana* sp.
Liriope	*Liriope* sp.
Moss sandwort	*Arenaria verna caespitosa*
Snow-in-summer	*Cerastium tomentosum*
Stonecrop	*Sedum* sp.
Thrift	*Armeria maritima*
Verbena	*Verbena bipinnatifida*
Woolly yarrow	*Achillea tomentosa*

Ground covers for patio and walkway crevices

The ideal ground cover for filling crevices in the walkway or spaces between bricks and flagstones is low, matted, and tolerant of traffic. It is wise to fill such spaces with an attractive ground cover plant in order to prevent the growth of weeds or lawn grasses. Among the best ground covers for use around paving stones or in similar crevices are:

Babystears	*Helxine soleirolii*
Bluets	*Houstonia caerulea*
Cinquefoil	*Potentilla tridentata*
Creeping mint	*Mentha requienii*
Dichondra	*Dichondra carolinensis*
Moss sandwort	*Arenaria verna caespitosa*
New Zealand bur	*Acaena microphylla*
Snow-in-summer	*Cerastium tomentosum*
Speedwell	*Veronica repens*
Woolly yarrow	*Achillea tomentosa*
Zoysiagrass	*Zoysia matrella*

Santolina is at home in hot, dry situations. Not only is it a favorite for covering rocky areas but santolina also grows well in the crevices of stone walls.

Trimmed

Untrimmed

Cinquefoil (*Potentilla* sp.) is excellent for planting between cracks in pavement. It will require occasional trimming, however.

Planting A Ground Cover

Initial preparation of the planting bed is the single most important factor in setting a ground cover. In most cases, this means thorough tilling of the entire area as for a lawn bed. In situations where the surface can't be tilled, as in rocky areas or over exposed tree roots, individual planting holes must be dug and organic matter, fertilizer, and other soil amendments mixed into the soil.

Ground covers can be planted at any time during the growing season, but spring planting is best for most areas of the country. In mild regions, such as zones 8, 9, and 10, fall planting is also satisfactory.

Space ground cover plants so they will cover the site as quickly as possible. Place small plants, such as carpet bugle or periwinkle, 6 to 12 inches apart. Place larger plants, such as juniper or cotoneaster, 2 to 4 feet apart. Closer planting will cover the ground more rapidly, but the additional plants required may be costly.

The following chart shows the area that 100 plants will cover when spaced at various intervals:

Planting distance (Inches)	*Area Covered (Square feet)*
4	11
6	25
8	44
10	70
12	100
18	225
24	400
36	900
48	1600

Preparing a large bed

Turn the soil with a roto-tiller to a depth of 6 to 10 inches, eradicating all grasses and weeds. Mix in generous quantities of organic matter such as compost, rotted sawdust, shredded leaves, shredded pine bark, grass clippings, or peat

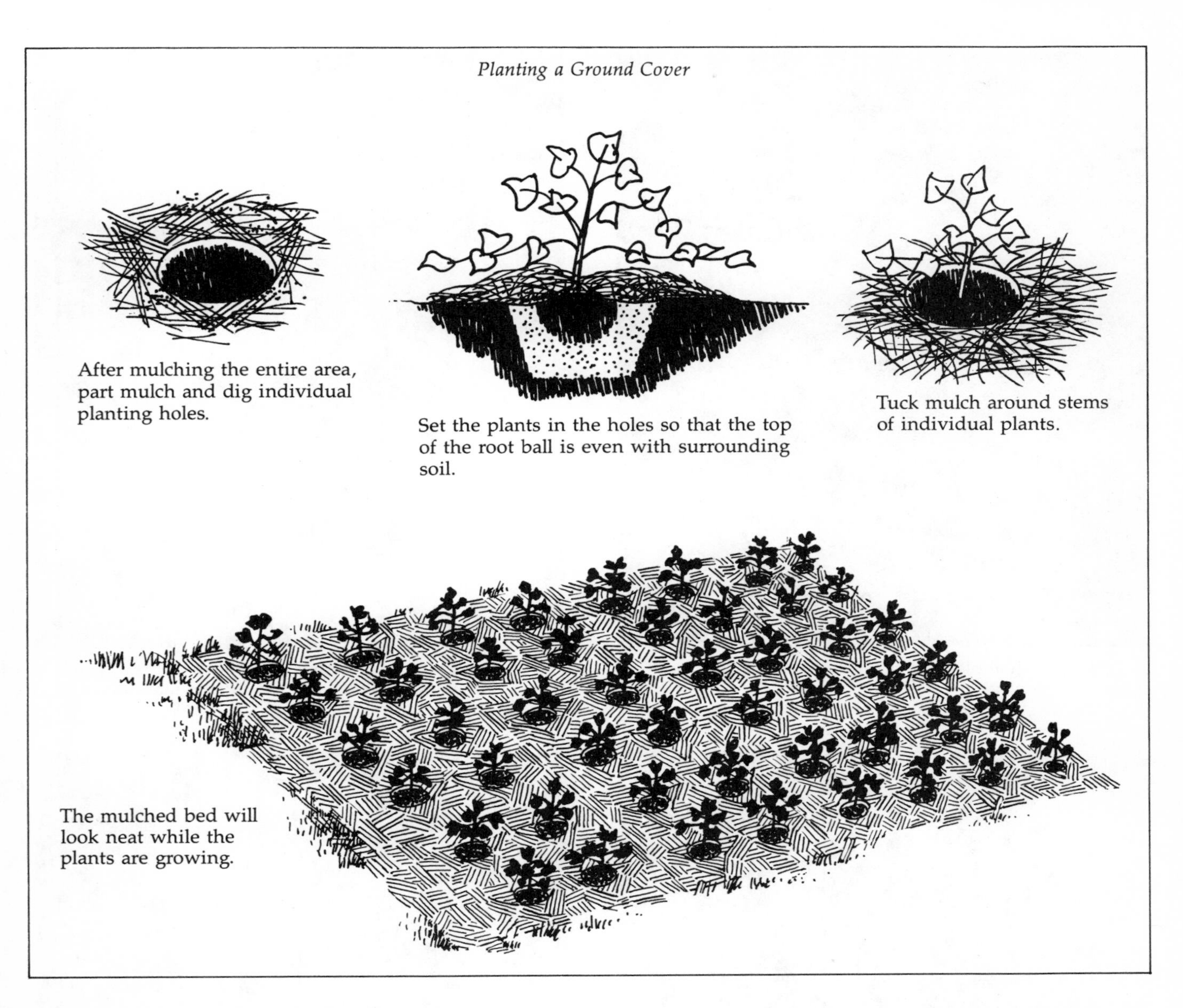

Planting a Ground Cover

moss. If you have not had the soil tested, broadcast complete fertilizer, such as 8–8–8 or 10–10–10, at the rate of 10 to 15 pounds per 1,000 square feet. If a soil test indicates a need for lime, add ground limestone at the recommended rate. Till the bed until the soil together with everything you have added is a smooth, crumbly homogeneous texture.

Cover the tilled bed with 3 to 4 inches of organic mulch such as pine straw, hay, cottonseed hulls, shredded pine bark, or similar material. This will maintain the fine texture of the soil and retard the growth of weeds until you actually set out plants. Spread the mulch as evenly as possible.

Using pruning shears, snip the growing tips of each plant. This will encourage branching and hasten coverage of the planting area.

Push back the mulch around each planting hole. With a trowel dig planting holes about 15 inches apart in all directions. Spacing may vary, however, depending on the plants you use and how fast you want the area covered. Firm the soil around each root ball and then water each plant thoroughly. If the soil around the balls forms a depression due to settling, add more soil to compensate. Pin stems of plants to the ground to stimulate root formation along the stems. Tuck mulch around the stem of each plant and water each plant individually.

A. Dig individual planting holes and mix fertilizer and organic matter into the soil.

C. Tip plastic pots upside down to remove plants. If you buy plants in metal containers, ask the nurseryman to slit the sides of the container.

B. Water plants lightly to make the root ball stay together and facilitate removal from the container.

D. Water each plant after setting it in the hole. The top of the root ball should be level with the surrounding soil.

E. Apply mulch before or after planting to conserve moisture, prevent erosion, and discourage weeds. Good mulch materials include hay, pine straw, and rotted sawdust.

Planting on a slope

Heavy mulching (4 to 6 inches deep) is sufficient for holding ground cover plants and soil in place. Do not use plastic mulches on slopes; plastic mulch encourages severe water run-off.

Low banks can be planted with no special preparation beyond that described for planting on untillable surfaces. If the slope or bank is steep, a simple retaining wall or series of retaining walls will facilitate the establishment of a ground cover. Plants can then be trained to cascade over the retaining wall.

Sloping areas are usually dry, so it is wise to select ground cover plants that can tolerate periodic drought. Large, vigorous plants such as junipers and contoneasters are ideal for sunny slopes.

Dig planting holes 24 to 48 inches apart, depending on how quickly you want the area covered. Mix organic matter and fertilizer into the soil to be used as backfill for each hole. Set plants and replace the backfill, firming the soil around each plant. Water thoroughly. Apply a 4- to 6-inch layer of mulch to prevent erosion, control weeds, and retain soil moisture. To be on the safe side, anchor the mulch with bird netting or strips of burlap. Peg burlap or netting down at each end and at one or two points near the middle.

Annual Care of Ground Cover Plants

Plants that are mulched will need little or no watering. In dry areas, water every 7 to 10 days if there is no rain. Mulch also discourages weeds.

Apply fertilizer in March. Liquid fertilizers are easier to apply and will reduce the danger of fertilizer burn. Fertilizers in pelleted form are also suited to ground covers. Generally speaking, ground covers require only a minimum of fertilizing. About ½ cup of fertilizer per 100 square feet is plenty for most plants.

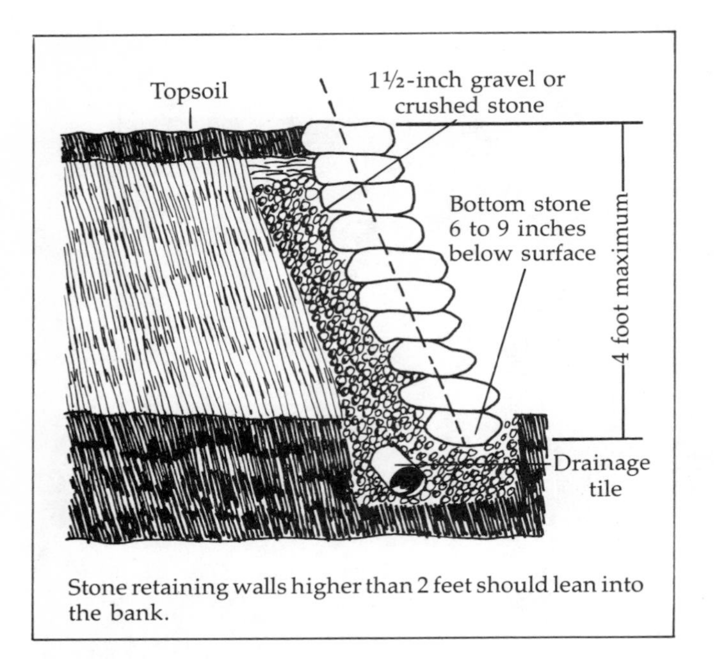

Stone retaining walls higher than 2 feet should lean into the bank.

If plants are left unmulched, be careful removing weeds. Ground covers are often shallow rooted and the roots may be damaged if they are disturbed in the weeding process. Do not use a hoe or other sharp instrument—pull the weeds by hand. Even better, be sure the planting beds are weed free before setting out plants.

Most ground covers are pruned only to remove dead wood or to keep the planting in bounds. The latter is especially true for creeping or vine-like plants.

In cooler areas, ground covers may suffer some cold damage. In places where the temperature drops but there is no permanent snow cover, frost heaves may force the plants out of the ground. A heavy winter mulch can help this situation because mulch reduces extreme soil temperature fluctuation.

You can also reduce winter damage by covering the plants with a moisture-conserving spray

Ground covers, such as carpet bugle (*Ajuga reptans*), that spread by underground stems can invade the lawn. The metal edging shown here is 12 inches deep.

Burlap mat that has not been treated with a preservative will hold soil and plants in place on a slope while ground cover becomes established. The burlap will eventually decompose in the soil.

Polypropylene netting, available through commercial sources, is another useful material for holding plantings on slopes. Make an *X*-shaped slit in the netting over each plant.

Slip the netting over each plant and tuck it around the stem.

Inspect plants regularly for insect pests. Most chewing and sucking insects feed on the undersides of leaves. Aphids, shown here, are perhaps the most common insect pest of ornamental plants.

which is available at many garden supply stores. In the event of severe winter damage, prune out damaged plants in the spring.

Most ground covers are free of insect pests. If an infestation becomes apparent, however, first try removing insects by spraying them off with a strong spray from the garden hose. If the insects return or if the infestation worsens, try to identify the insect; then select the appropriate insecticide. Call the county agricultural extension agent for advice on selecting and using insecticides. Recommendations change frequently and the county agent has the most up-to-date information concerning pesticides.

Propagating Ground Cover Plants

Cuttings

Most ground cover plants are easy to propagate from cuttings taken during the growing season. With a sharp knife, take cuttings from the tips of plants. Cuttings should be 3 to 6 inches long. A mixture of equal parts sand and peat moss is an excellent rooting medium. Prepared potting and rooting soils are available at garden supply stores. Spread the medium in a rooting flat or in individual peat pots. Water the medium gently to settle it.

Dip the stem end of the cutting in rooting hormone powder, such as Rootone, and insert the cutting in the medium. Poke a hole in the medium with a pencil to avoid removing hormone powder as you insert the cutting. If you do not use rooting hormone, insert the cutting directly into the medium. Remove only the foliage that would be below the surface. Firm the medium around the cuttings and place the flat or peat pots in a lightly shaded area and cover with glass or clear polyethylene plastic. Keep the medium as moist as a damp sponge.

Root formation should begin in 2 to 4 weeks. Test cuttings by pulling gently at them. Those with roots will be more secure than those without roots. When rooting begins, poke a few holes in the plastic or raise the glass cover slightly to let in air. Gradual exposure of the cuttings will help them to "harden-off," that is, become accustomed to a normal outdoor growing environment.

Rooted cuttings should be transplanted to a well-prepared bed.

Divisions

Mature clumps of ground cover plants may be divided in late summer and fall in the South. In cooler areas, make divisions in the spring. Peel apart the vigorous, outer portions of the clumps and discard the centers. Leave 3 to 5 shoots in each clump; do not overdivide. Transplant the new clumps where they are needed.

Propagating Ground Cover Plants From Cuttings

A. Fill a shallow box with peat pots and fill the pots with a mixture of equal parts peat moss and sand (or perlite).

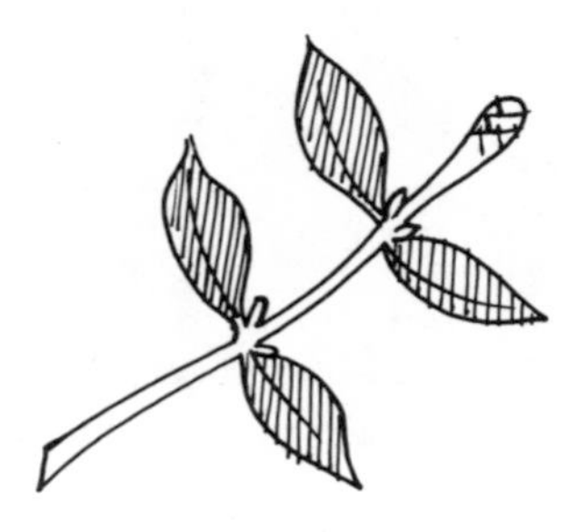

B. Take cuttings of healthy plants with a sharp knife. Cuttings should be 4 to 6 inches long.

C. Remove lower leaves from the cutting.

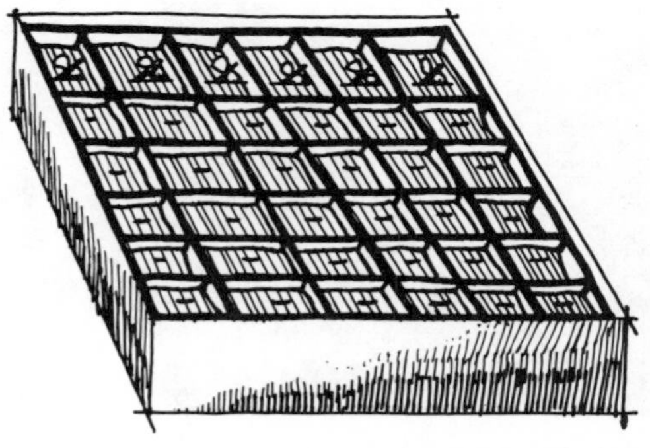

D. Insert the cuttings in the peat pots and place the flat in a shady place. Keep the rooting soil moist at all times. Depending on the kind of plant, root formation will take place in 2 to 6 weeks.

Propagating Ground Covers From Divisions

A. Dig up crowded clumps of plants.

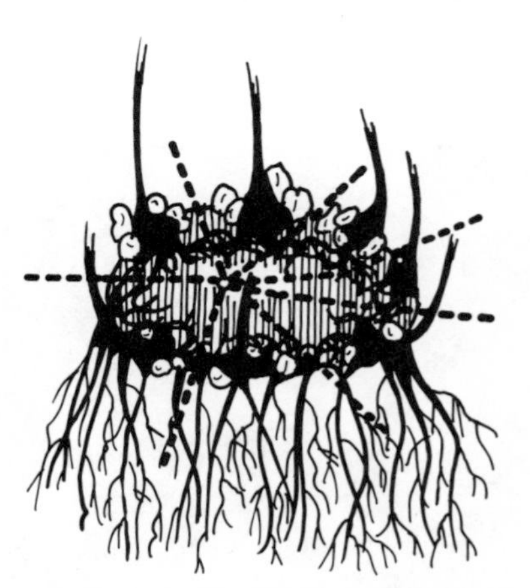

B. Gently hose soil off the roots. Select divisions with tiny growth buds clustered at the base of the old stems. Pull the divisions apart with your fingers or use a sharp knife.

C. Transplant divisions with several growth buds to desired locations. Discard the center of the clump as well as the sickly divisions with only one or no growth buds.

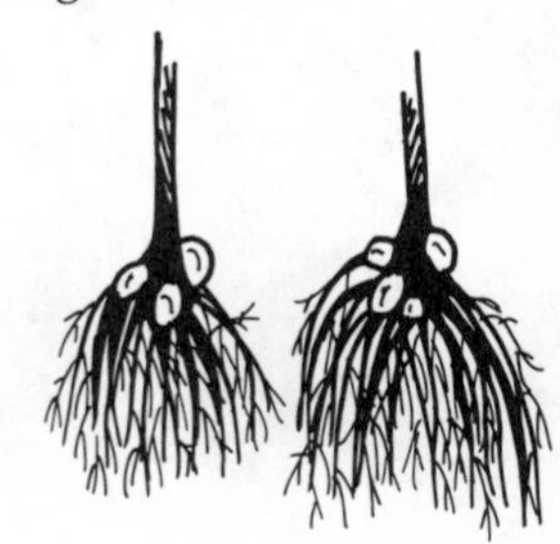

Popular ground covers

Three levels of ground cover plant here include: Aaronsbeard (*Hypericum* sp.) along the wall, Asiatic jasmine (*Trachelospernum* sp.) on the intermediate level, and mondograss (*Ophiopogon* sp.) along the sidewalk.

Sprenger asparagus (*Asparagus sprengerii*) is an attractive, billowy ground cover in small areas.

Ajuga, also known as carpet bugle, is an excellent ground cover around rocks.

Japanese honeysuckle (*Lonicera japonica*), confined to a desired area, makes an excellent, fast spreading ground cover. Allowed to grow rampantly, however, it becomes a pest.

Ajuga, planted around the bricks of this walk, define the pathway through a bed of asiatic jasmine and prevent the latter from invading the path.

English ivy (*Hedera helix*), an old reliable among ground covers, is most at home in large plantings.

This small bed of English ivy gives an impression of depth to the patio.

Shore juniper (*Juniperus conferta*) is a good choice for small or large areas.

As an underplanting for these tree-form hollies, pachysandra softens lines between the wall and the lawn.

GROUND COVER SELECTION GUIDE

Common Names	*Botanical Name*	*Hardiness Range*	*Height (inches)*	*Rate of Spread/ Method*	*Light Requirements*	*Soil*	*Foliage**	*Flower Color*	*Time of Bloom*
Aaronsbeard, St. Johnswort	*Hypericum* sp.	4–8	16–20	Medium/subsurface stolons	Full sun to light shade	Almost any	E-south D-north	Yellow	Summer
American barrenwort	*Vancouveria* sp.	5–8	12–15	Medium/tufts	Light to deep shade	Moist/drained loamy	E-south D-north	White	Late spring
Asiatic jasmine	*Trachelospermum asiaticum*	7–10	Prostrate vine	Medium/surface stems	Full sun to medium shade	Almost any well drained	E	Yellow	Late spring
Babystears	*Helxine soleirolii*	8–10	Prostrate vine	Slow/surface creepers	Medium to deep shade	Moist/tol. acid	E	—	—
Barrenwort	*Epimedium* sp.	3–8	6–10	Medium/surface rhizomes	Full sun to deep shade	Moist/peaty acid	E-south D-north	Pink/violet yellow/white	Spring
Beach wormwood	*Artemisia stelleriana*	2–8	18–24	Fast/surface runners	Full sun	Dry/sandy infertile	D	—	—
Bearberry	*Arctostaphylos uva-ursi*	2–7	10–14	Slow/prostrate creeping shrub	Full sun to light shade	Almost any	E	White	Late spring
Bergenia	*Bergenia* sp.	4–7	10–12	Medium/subsurface rootstocks	Full sun to medium shade	Moist/drained loamy	D	Pink/purple white	Early spring
Birdsfoot trefoil	*Lotus corniculatus*	4–8	6–12	Fast/trailing stems	Full sun to light shade	Dry/loamy or poor	D	Yellow	Summer & fall
Blue fescue	*Festuca ovina glauca*	3–7	6–8	Slow to medium/ tufts	Full sun to light shade	Dry/sandy poor	E	—	—
Bluets	*Houstonia caerulea*	1–7	4–8	Fast/surface runners	Light to deep shade	Moist/peaty acid	D	Blue/yellow centers	Spring
Carolina jessamine	*Gelsemium sempervirens*	7–9	Creeping vine	Medium/surface creeper	Full sun to light shade	Almost any; prefers loamy	E	Yellow	Early spring
Carpet bugle	*Ajuga reptans*	3–8	4–10	Rapid/surface runners	Full sun to medium shade	Moist/loamy drained	E-south D-north	Pink/blue white	Late spring
Cinquefoil	*Potentilla tridentata*	2–7	2–12	Medium/creeping rootstock	Full sun to light shade	Dry-moist/ loamy/acid	E	Yellow/white (inconspicuous)	Late spring & summer
Coral bells	*Heuchera sanguinea*	3–8	12–18	Medium/subsurface rootstocks	Full sun to light shade	Moist/loamy drained	E	Red/pink white	Spring to midsummer

*E indicates evergreen, D indicates deciduous

GROUND COVER SELECTION GUIDE

Common Names	*Botanical Name*	*Hardiness Range*	*Height (inches)*	*Rate of Spread/ Method*	*Light Requirements*	*Soil*	*Foliage**	*Flower Color*	*Time of Bloom*
Cotoneaster	*Cotoneaster* sp.	5–9	12–36	Slow to medium/ branch tips root when touching soil	Full sun to medium shade	Any drained/ tolerates dry	E or D	Pink/white	Early summer (red berries in fall & winter)
Cowberry	*Vaccinium vitis-idaea*	3–7	10–12	Slow/subsurface stolons	Light to deep shade	Moist/peaty acid	E	Pink	Summer
Crested iris	*Iris cristata*	2–8	6–8	Slow to medium surface rhizomes	Full sun to medium shade	Moist loamy/ tol. acid	D	Blue/white	Early summer
Daylily	*Hemerocallis* sp.	2–10	12–36	Slow to medium/ divide roots	Full sun to light shade	Almost any	D	Red/rose/pink salmon/lavender bronze/orange yellow/bicolors	Spring to late summer
Dichondra	*Dichondra carolinensis*	7–10	2–3	Fast/subsurface runners	Full sun to medium shade	Moist/drained loamy	E	——	——
English ivy	*Hedera helix*	5–10	4–10	Medium/surface runners	Light to deep shade	Moist/drained tol. acid	E	——	——
Evergreen candytuft	*Iberis sempervirens*	3–9	8–12	Slow/subsurface rootstocks	Full sun to light shade	Moist/drained tol. acid	E	White	Early spring to summer
Fleeceflower	*Polygonum reynoutria*	5–9	10–12	Fast/subsurface stolons	Full sun to medium shade	Moist or dry loamy	D	Greenish white	Late summer
Foamflower	*Tiarella cordifolia*	4–8	10–12	Medium/subsurface rootstocks	Light to deep shade	Moist/peaty or loam/acid	D	White	Early spring
Forgetmenot	*Myosotis scorpioides*	3–8	8–12	Fast/self-seeding	Light to medium shade	Moist/drained loamy	D	Pink/blue white	Late spring to late summer
Fringed bleedingheart	*Dicentra eximia*	2–9	10–12	Slow/self-seeding	Full sun to medium shade	Moist/drained loamy	D	Red/pink white	Early spring & summer
Galax, Beetleweed	*Galax aphylla*	2–8	5–6	Slow/clumps	Light to deep shade	Moist/peaty acid	E	White	Summer
Gardenia, dwarf	*Gardenia radicans*	8–10	6–12	Slow/spreading branches	Full sun to light shade	Moist/peaty acid/drained	E	White	Early summer
Germander	*Teucrium chamaedrys*	4–7	10–12	Slow/surface creeping stems	Full sun to light shade	Dry/sandy tol. poor	E	Purple	Summer

GROUND COVER SELECTION GUIDE

Common Names	Botanical Name	Hardiness Range	Height (inches)	Rate of Spread/ Method	Light Requirements	Soil	Foliage*	Flower Color	Time of Bloom
Gill-over-the-ground, Ground-ivy	*Glecoma hederacea*	2–8	6–8	Fast/subsurface runners	Full sun to medium shade	Almost any	D	Purple	Summer
Gold-dust Basket-of-gold	*Alyssum saxatile*	4–8	10–12	Slow to medium/ clumps	Full sun	Average/loamy drained	D	Yellow	Spring
Heath	*Erica carnea*	5–7	4–16	Medium/creeping rootstock	Full sun to light shade	Dry/sandy peat	E	Red/pink white	Spring
Heather	*Calluna vulgaris*	4–7	4–24	Slow to medium/ creeping rootstock	Full sun to light shade	Dry/sandy peat	E	Red/pink purple/lavender white	Summer
Honeysuckle	*Lonicera japonica*	5–10	Prostrate vine	Fast/surface & subsurface runners	Full sun to deep shade	Almost any	E	Yellow or white	Spring
Juniper									
Creeping	*Juniperus horizontalis*	2–9	12–18	Medium/stem tips root in soil	Full sun to light shade	dry/sandy tol. poor or acid	E	—	—
Prostrate	*J. communis depressa*	2–9	24–36				E	—	—
Shore	*J. conferta*	5–9	10–12				E	—	—
Kenilworth ivy, Wall toadflax	*Cymbalaria muralis*	5–10	4–6	Fast/surface runners	Light to medium shade	Moist/loamy tol. alkaline	D	Mauve/blue with yellow throats	Spring to fall
Lantana, trailing	*Lantana montevidensis*	8–10	12–18	Fast/trailing surface stems	Full sun	Dry/sandy or loamy/poor	D	Pink/lavender yellow/white	Summer & fall
Lentenrose	*Helleborus orientalis*	6–9	15–20	Medium/divisions	Light to medium shade	Moist/peaty drained/tol. acid	E	Purple/rose	Late winter to spring
Lilyofthevalley	*Convallaria majalis*	2–8	4–6	Fast/subsurface runners	Full sun to deep shade	Almost any	D	Pink/white	Spring
Liriope, Lilyturf	*Liriope* sp.	5–10	8–16	Medium/tufts or subsurface stolons	Full sun to deep shade	Almost any	E	Blue/white	Summer
Mint, creeping	*Mentha requienii*	5–9	1–2	Medium/subsurface runners	Full sun to deep shade	Moist/loamy tol. acid	D-north E-south	—	—
Mock strawberry	*Duchesnea indica*	3–9	2	Fast/surface runners or seed	Full sun to deep shade	Moist/drained loamy/tol. acid	D	Yellow (red berries)	Spring (summer)

GROUND COVER SELECTION GUIDE

Common Names	*Botanical Name*	*Hardiness Range*	*Height (inches)*	*Rate of Spread/ Method*	*Light Requirements*	*Soil*	*Foliage**	*Flower Color*	*Time of Bloom*
Monkeygrass Mondograss	*Ophiopogon japonicus*	5–10	6–12	Slow/tufts or subsurface stolons	Full sun to medium shade	Moist/drained loamy/acid	E	Lavender (black berries)	Early summer (late summer & fall)
Moss sandwort, Irish moss	*Arenaria verna caespitosa*	2–8	10–12	Medium to fast/ subsurface runners	Full sun to medium shade	Moist/drained sandy loam	E	—	—
New Zealand bur	*Acaena microphylla*	6–10	1–2	Slow/subsurface runners	Full sun	Moist or dry/ drained/tol. alkaline	E	—	—
Pachistima	*Pachistima canbyi*	5–7	6–12	Slow/subsurface stems	Full sun to medium shade	Moist/peaty acid	E	—	—
Pachysandra, Japanese spurge	*Pachysandra terminalis*	4–8	6–8	Fast/subsurface runners	Light to deep shade	Moist/peaty tol. acid	E	White	Spring
Partridgeberry	*Mitchella repens*	3–8	2–3	Medium/surface runners	Light to deep shade	Moist/peaty acid	E	Pinkish white	Early summer
Periwinkle, Myrtle	*Vinca* sp.	3–10	6–10	Fast/subsurface stolons	Light to deep shade	Moist/loamy tol. acid	E	Purple/blue white	Early spring
Phlox									
Blue phlox	*Phlox divaricata*	3–9	10–12	Medium/creeping stems	Full sun to light shade	Average	D	Blue/lavender	Spring
Moss pink	*P. subulata*	2–9	6–8	Fast/surface runners	Full sun	Almost any	E	Red/pink/ purple/lavender	Late spring; some vars. repeat bloom in fall
Pinks	*Dianthus* sp.	2–10	6–12	Medium or tufts seed or creeping stems	Full sun	Avg./drained tol. alkaline	E	Red/pink lavender/white	Spring & summer
Plantainlily	*Hosta* sp.	5–9	12–36	Slow/clumps	Full sun to medium shade	Average/ drained	D	Purple/blue white	Summer to early fall
Rockcress	*Arabis* sp.	3–8	4–10	Medium/creeping surface stems	Full sun	Average to dry/tol. poor	D or E	White	Spring
Santolina, Lavender cotton	*Santolina chamaecyparissus*	6–10	18–24	Fast/spreading branches	Full sun to light shade	Almost any/tol. poor/prefers drained	E	Yellow	Summer
Snow-in-summer	*Cerastium tomentosum*	2–9	6–8	Fast/surface & subsurface stems & seed	Full sun to medium shade	Average to dry/tol. poor	E	White	Summer

GROUND COVER SELECTION GUIDE

Common Names	*Botanical Name*	*Hardiness Range*	*Height (inches)*	*Rate of Spread/ Method*	*Light Requirements*	*Soil*	*Foliage**	*Flower Color*	*Time of Bloom*
Speedwell	*Veronica repens*	4–8	4–6	Fast/subsurface rootstocks	Full sun to medium shade	Moist/drained tol. acid	E	Bluish white	Spring
Star jasmine, Confederate jasmine	*Trachelospermum jasminoides*	7–10	Prostrate vine	Medium/surface stems	Full sun to medium shade	Almost any	E	White	Late spring & summer
Stonecrop	*Sedum* sp.	2–10	3–12	Fast/surface runners	Full sun to light shade	Average to dry/tol. poor	E	Red/pink/purple yellow/white	Spring to fall
Strawberry geranium	*Saxifraga sarmentosa*	6–9	3–4	Medium/creeping stems	Light shade	Almost any/ tol. poor & acid	E	Pink/white	Early summer
Sweet woodruff	*Asperula odorata*	4–8	6–8	Fast/subsurface runners	Medium to deep shade	Moist/peaty tol. acid	E	White	Early spring
Thrift	*Armeria maritima*	1–9	4–10	Medium/clumps	Full sun	Average to dry/tol. poor	D	Pink/white	Spring
Verbena	*Verbena bipinnatifida*	2–9	8–12	Fast/creeping stems	Full sun to light shade	Dry/sandy or average/ tol. poor	D	Red/purple	Spring to fall
Violets	*Viola* sp.	2–9	4–18	Fast/subsurface runners/self-seeding	Light to deep shade	Average or moist/drained	D-north E-south	Nearly all colors	Spring or summer; some vars. repeat bloom in fall
Wild ginger	*Asarum* sp.	4–8	4–6	Medium/surface creeping rootstocks	Light to deep shade	Moist/peaty/ acid	D or E	—	—
Wintercreeper	*Euonymus fortunei*	4–9	2–12	Slow/creeping stems	Full sun to deep shade	Moist/peaty acid	E	—	—
Wintergreen	*Gaultheria procumbens*	3–8	2–5	Slow/subsurface stolons	Light to medium shade	Moist/peaty acid	E	White	Late spring
Wooly yarrow	*Achillea tomentosa*	2–9	4–6	Fast/creeping stems	Full sun to medium shade	Dry/tol. poor	E	Pink/yellow white	Summer

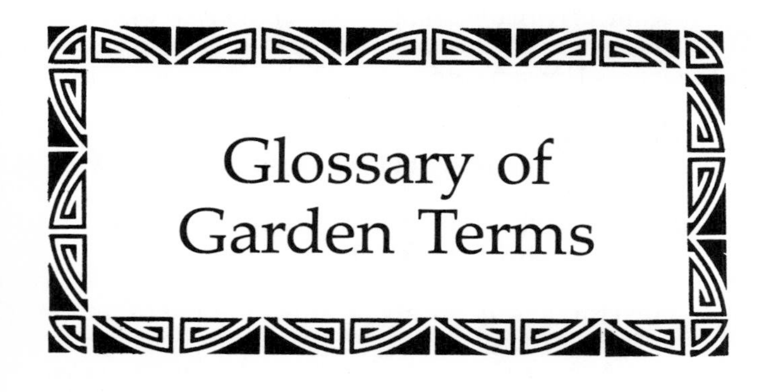

Acid soil—Soil with a pH reading of 1.0 to 6.9, called "sour soil" in former times.
Aeration, aerating—The process of allowing air to penetrate and circulate in the soil.
Alkaline soil—Soil with a pH reading of 7.1 to 14.0, called "sweet soil" in former times.
Annual—A plant which completes its entire life cycle of germination, growth, flower, and seed production in 1 year and then dies.
Bed—An area in which soil has been prepared for planting.
Broadcast—To distribute by hand, as with fertilizer or grass seed.
Chemical fertilizer—Fertilizer manufactured from mineral or other inorganic chemical compounds.
Compaction (of soil)—Packing down of soil by rain or traffic.
Complete fertilizer—Any fertilizer that contains some measure of all three primary fertilizing elements: nitrogen, phosphorous, and potassium.
Compost—Decomposed plant matter that has undergone a fermentation process while decomposing.
Cool-season grass—A lawn grass that makes its strongest growth during the cool seasons of spring and fall, then becomes partially dormant (inactive) during hot summer weather. The fescues, bents, and bluegrasses are cool-season grasses.
Cultural requirements—Climate, soil, light, moisture, and other conditions that influence the vital processes of plant growth.
Cutting—A portion of plant, usually a piece of stem or root, from which a new plant may be grown.
Deciduous—Characterized by the loss of leaves during the dormant season.
Dethatching—The process of removing the layer of partially decayed roots and grass clippings that collect on the soil surface of the lawn and impede water and air penetration to the roots.
Division—The breaking apart of root clumps to grow new plants.
Dormant, dormancy—At rest; a period of inactivity following the growing season. Deciduous plants lose their leaves in the fall as they enter dormancy in winter.
Drainage—The ability of soil to allow water to drain through rather than to collect on the surface.
Edging—A surface-level separation between planting beds and lawns, usually made from wood, concrete, stone, brick, or other materials that prohibit the spread of plants by underground stems. Chemical herbicides can also be used for this purpose.
Erosion—The washing away of soil by rain or wind.
Evergreen—Retaining leaves throughout the year.
Fertilizer burn—Damage caused to plants, especially young plants, by excessive fertilizer.
Flat—A shallow container used for growing plants from seed to be transplanted later or for rooting cuttings to obtain new plants.
Friable—Loose, porous; usually in reference to soil texture.
Frost heaves—Ridges or mounds caused by repeated freezing and thawing of the soil.
Fungicide—A material used for destroying fungi.
Germinate, germination—The earliest stage of growth from seed, when the seed opens and a new plant begins to form.
Grading—The process of leveling an area of ground.
Ground cover—Any plant used to cover the ground. Lawn grasses are the most commonly used ground cover plants.
Growth habit—The height, spread, and form of a plant.
Hardening off—The process of gradually acclimating a plant to a change of environment so that the shock of the new environment does not cause unnecessary stress to the plant.
Hardy, hardiness—The ability of a plant to withstand cold.
Herbaceous—Having a supple herblike character as opposed to a woody character.
Herbicide—A chemical material used for killing plants.
Humus—Decaying organic matter in soil.
Hybrid—A plant that results from crossing two or more parent plants from different species or varieties.
Insecticide—Any material used for killing insects.
Iron chlorosis—Iron deficiency in plants that results in yellowed leaves with leaf veins usually remaining green.
Leach—In reference to soils, leach means drain or wash through the soil.
Leggy—Characterized by elongated stems with stunted leaves; often caused by inadequate sunlight.
Lime, liming—A lime-derived product, such as ground limestone, added to the soil to raise the soil pH and thus relieve excessive acidity.
Mass planting—A planting in which plants are grouped thickly together.
Mulch—Any material which is spread on the soil around the base of a plant to conserve moisture, prevent soil compaction, and hamper the growth

of weeds. Common mulching materials include grass clippings, leaf mold, rotted sawdust, shredded bark, wood chips, compost, pine straw, and black polyethylene plastic.

Organic fertilizer—A fertilizer derived from decaying animal or plant material. Common organic fertilizers include manure, cottonseed meal, bone meal, dried blood, and sewage sludge.

Organic matter—Decaying plant material which is added to the soil to improve soil structure, drainage, and prevent soil compaction. Pine straw, hay, grass clippings, sawdust, sugarcane pulp, shredded bark, peat moss, and other decaying materials are suitable for this purpose.

Overseeding—Distributing cool-season grass seed, such as annual rye, over common Bermudagrass in the fall to maintain green color while the Bermuda goes dormant for the winter and turns brown.

Peat moss—partially decomposed sphagnum moss, noted for its moisture retaining capacity. Peat moss can hold 6 to 12 times its dry weight in water.

Perennial—A plant that lives for 3 years or more.

Pesticide—Any material used to kill pests such as insects, fungus disease organisms, or weeds.

pH—The scale for measuring soil acidity. On a scale of 1.0 to 14.0, 7.0 represents a neutral (neither acid nor alkaline) state. Below 7.0 the soil is acid (sour) and above 7.0 the soil is alkaline (sweet).

Plug—A small section of turf, usually 2 or 3 inches square. Plugs of spreading grasses planted at 1- to 2-foot intervals will cover an entire lawn area in one or two growing seasons, depending on the type of grass, soil, and climate.

Postemergence herbicide—An herbicide used to control weeds that have already appeared above ground.

Preemergence herbicide—An herbicide used to prevent weeds before the seeds can germinate and produce top growth.

Propagate—To produce new plants, either from seeds or from the vegetative parts of a plant (stems, roots, leaves).

Pruning—The process of removing parts of a plant to stimulate new growth, to train to a desired form, or to eliminate dead or diseased growth.

Resistance, resistant varieties—The natural ability of a plant to withstand attack by insect pests or diseases. Some plant varieties have greater natural resistance to attack than others.

Rhizome—An enlarged portion of underground stem in which some plants store nutrients. Many plants spread by sending up new top growth from these underground stems.

Rooting hormone—A chemical that stimulates root formation on cuttings of plants.

Rotary tiller, roto-tiller—A machine that turns the soil by means of powered revolving arms called *tynes*.

Runner—An above ground, prostrate branch that forms roots at the joints or tip when it comes in contact with the soil. Common English ivy (*Hedera helix*) spreads by this method.

Scalping—Uneven cutting of grass, usually caused by a bent or unbalanced mower blade. Scalped areas temporarily turn yellow but should revive.

Sod—Sections of turf with lawn grass already growing in them.

Soil amendments—Any material added to the soil to improve structure, fertility, or pH.

Soil test—An analysis of a sample of soil performed to determine soil fertility, acidity, and the presence of nematodes, soil insects, and disease organisms.

Spore—A one-celled reproductive body. Fungi, ferns, and mosses reproduce by spores.

Sprig—A single grass plant used to propagate additional plants when set in prepared soil.

Stolon—A prostrate stem that grows either above ground or just below the surface and produces new plants at its tip.

Thatch—A layer of partially decayed grass roots and leaves that collects on the soil surface in lawns, especially when clippings are not regularly removed after mowing. The thatch layer can impede moisture penetration and air circulation in the soil. Remove thatch annually.

Topdress—To apply fertilizer or other soil additives to the soil surface without raking them into the soil.

Topsoil—The topmost layer of soil, ideally rich in humus and organic matter.

Trace elements—Minor fertilizing elements necessary to plant growth in addition to the three primary agents, nitrogen, phosphorous, and potassium. Important trace elements include magnesium, calcium, boron, and iron.

Turf—A dense mat of lawn grass foliage, roots, and soil.

Variegated foliage—Characterized by stripes, blotches, or margins of a color other than green, usually white.

Variety—The subdivision of a species; a group of individual plants within a species which are distinct in form or minor characteristics.

Vegetative planting—Planting parts other than seeds; usually cuttings of stems or roots.

Warm-season grass—A lawn grass that makes its strongest growth during the warmest months of the year, then becomes dormant in the fall. The Bermudas, zoysias, St. Augustine, carpetgrass, and centipedegrass are warm-season grasses.

Weed—A plant, desirable or otherwise, growing in an undesirable place. Thus, Bermudagrass becomes a weed in a St. Augustine lawn.

Weep holes—Drainage holes in a retaining wall.

Wilt—A sagging of leaves and stems of plants due to a loss of moisture through transpiration. Several fungus diseases also cause wilting.

Woody—Having a woodlike character, as a tree or shrub.

Index